Growing in God's Word

Bill Bright
Joette Whims and Melody Hunskor

NewLife
PUBLICATIONS

Growing in God's Word
Children's Discipleship Series, Book 3

Published by
New*Life* Publications
A ministry of Campus Crusade for Christ
P.O. Box 620877
Orlando, FL 32862-0877

Edited by Lynn Copeland
Design and production by Genesis Group
Illustrations by Bruce Day
Cover by David Marty Design

Printed in the United States of America

ISBN 1-56399-153-5

Unless indicated otherwise, Scripture quotations are from the *New International Version,* © 1973, 1978, 1984 by the International Bible Society. Published by Zondervan Bible Publishers, Grand Rapids, Michigan.

Scripture quotations designated TLB are from *The Living Bible,* © 1971 by Tyndale House Publishers, Inc., Wheaton, Illinois.

Scripture quotations designated NLT are from the *New Living Translation,* © 1996 by Tyndale House Publishers, Inc., Wheaton, Illinois.

For more information, write:
Campus Crusade for Christ International—100 Lake Hart Drive, Orlando, FL 32832, USA
L.I.F.E., Campus Crusade for Christ—P.O. Box 40, Flemington Markets, 2129, Australia
Campus Crusade for Christ of Canada—Box 529, Sumas, WA 98295
Campus Crusade for Christ—Fairgate House, King's Road, Tyseley, Birmingham, B11 2AA, United Kingdom
Lay Institute for Evangelism, Campus Crusade for Christ—P.O. Box 8786, Auckland, 1035, New Zealand
Campus Crusade for Christ—9 Lock Road #3-03, PacCan Centre, Singapore
Great Commission Movement of Nigeria—P.O. Box 500, Jos, Plateau State, Nigeria, West Africa

Contents

Why a Discipleship Series for Children? 5
How to Use the Lessons 9
The Exciting World of the 9- to 12-Year-Old 13
Tips for Teaching Your Students 15

Unit One: What Is the Bible?

LESSON 1: Book of Books 23
LESSON 2: Perfect Puzzle 35
LESSON 3: Our Treasure 49
LESSON 4: Book of Wisdom 63

Unit Two: What's in the Old Testament?

LESSON 5: The Drama Begins 83
LESSON 6: Law and Grace 97
LESSON 7: Joshua and David 111
LESSON 8: Elijah and Jeremiah 123

Unit Three: What's in the New Testament?

LESSON 9: The Story of Jesus 141
LESSON 10: The Story of the Church 155
LESSON 11: The Church Grows 167
LESSON 12: The End of the Story 179
LESSON 13: Jesus and the Tabernacle 193

Resources 205
Certificate of Participation 207

Why a Discipleship Series for Children?

Our children are our greatest assets. In God's eyes, they are a heritage and a reward (Psalm 127:3). Whether you are a parent or a children's teacher, these preteens are the most vital resource you will ever have the privilege to touch.

Proverbs gives us the promise I am sure you have heard many times, "Train a child in the way he should go, and when he is old he will not turn from it" (22:6). What is God's method of training children? It is not to sit the child down and merely lecture him. God's method is a teach-as-you-go process. Before the Israelites entered the Promised Land, God instructed them how to teach their children His Word:

> Hear, O Israel! The LORD is our God, the LORD alone. And you must love the LORD your God with all your heart, all your soul, and all your strength. And you must commit yourselves wholeheartedly to these commands I am giving you today. Repeat them again and again to your children. Talk about them when you are at home and when you are away on a journey, when you are lying down and when you are getting up again. Tie them to your hands as a reminder, and wear them on your forehead. Write them on the doorposts of your house and on your gates (Deuteronomy 6:4–9, NLT).

The biblical pattern for learning is twofold: (1) children learn by watching, so adults must practice what they teach their children, by committing themselves wholeheartedly to God's commands; and (2) children learn by doing, by walking alongside a godly adult who lovingly and consistently guides them. This kind of teaching is deeply rooted in God's Word.

Children do best with active learning methods. The active learning method is basically what Jesus used in discipling His followers while He lived on this earth. Jesus not only preached to the crowds and taught through stories, He also emphasized all the truths He taught through example. The disciples saw how their Master patiently responded even when He was hungry and tired. They watched Him tenderly minister as the crowds pushed and shoved around Him. Their troubled hearts were soothed by His compassion, and their wrong attitudes received His gentle rebuke. They learned through situations they could see and touch, such as distributing the miraculously multiplied loaves of bread, experiencing a roaring sea become calm, and watching the diseased become whole. This was so much more effective for them than if they had simply heard Jesus say, "I can do anything." In the most moving demonstration of God's love, the disciples witnessed the horror of the crucifixion, which magnified the triumph and joy of the resurrection. Whatever Jesus taught, He lived and demonstrated to His disciples.

The Beginnings of the Series

Preteens are at a vulnerable time in their lives. They are changing rapidly. Your 9- and 10-year-old students may still regard you as a hero, whereas your 11- and 12-year-olds may question your authority. But this age is still relatively peaceful compared to the physical, emotional, and mental tumult these children will experience during their teen years. The preteen years are a marvelous time to give children a foundation in God's Word that they can use as they develop into adults.

The lessons in this book will help you harness the curiosity your students have about life. Your students are still young enough to enjoy the activities, but old enough to begin grasping some of the deeper and more abstract concepts of the Christian life.

The adult version of this material, *Ten Basic Steps Toward Christian Maturity*, has been used successfully around the world. The development of the Bible study series was a product of necessity. As the ministry of Campus Crusade for Christ expanded from the UCLA campus to scores of campuses across America, thousands of students committed their lives to Christ—several hundred on a single campus. A resource was needed to help them grow in their newfound faith.

In 1955, I asked several of my fellow staff to assist me in preparing Bible studies that would encourage both evangelism and spiritual growth in new believers. These studies would stimulate individuals and groups to explore the depths and riches of God's Word. *Ten Basic Steps Toward Christian Maturity* was the fruit of our combined labor.

Over the years since then, many believers have expressed a desire to teach these same biblical principles to their children. Some even adapted the adult version to do just that. They found that the basic principles taught in the adult series translated well to 9- to 12-year-olds.

Of course, discipling children is much different than teaching adults. You cannot sit children down with a Bible and lead a Bible study with them. Children need hands-on activities that will help them comprehend biblical principles. They need concrete examples and specific directions on how to apply the teachings to their life. This discipleship series was designed with their needs in mind.

How to Use the Series

This series of four books presents the basic doctrines and teachings of God's Word in a format that will attract your upper-elementary students. The books in this series can be used in two ways:

1. If you are going through the complete series, your students will begin with the previous book, *Beginning the Christian Adventure,* in which they will learn who Jesus is and how they can experience the life that Jesus has provided for each believer. The succeeding three books will teach:

   - *Discovering Our Awesome God*—Who God is and how He relates to us through His Holy Spirit

- *Growing in God's Word*—A basic overview of the Bible and how to study it for Christian growth

- *Building an Active Faith*—How to grow as a believer, including the importance of giving our whole selves to God, witnessing of His work in our life, and obeying Him

Each book will cover one-quarter of the year, and the complete series provides 52 lessons. By completing all four books, your students will have a well-rounded view of the Christian life.

2. Each book in the series is also designed to be used on its own. If you are not going on to the other three books, you will find that the units are complete in themselves.

I pray that these lessons will help you touch many children's lives for our Lord Jesus Christ. My prayer is that the upcoming generation will truly change our world for Christ!

How to Use the Lessons

Each lesson in this book is carefully crafted for an optimal learning experience. The lessons are built around several central themes:

- The *book objective* gives the overall purpose for the thirteen lessons.

- The *unit objective* defines how the unit will fit into the book's goal.

- The *lesson objective* shows what the learner will discover about God's message to us within the parameters of the book and unit goals.

- The *lesson application* describes what the learner should be able to do by the end of the lesson.

To accomplish the objectives and application, each lesson contains seven activities. Each builds on the previous activity to move the student to the application. Although the components may appear in different order, each lesson contains the following:

 Opening Activity: Usually a more active part of the lesson, this activity will grab your students' attention and help them begin focusing on the upcoming lesson objective.

 Bible Story: This story or Bible truth illustrates the main principle of the lesson. The story is presented in a way that will hold the attention of your students and engage them in the learning process. The Bible story develops the lesson objective.

 Lesson Activity: This hands-on activity involves the students in discovering more about the truths presented in the Bible story. The activity helps students begin applying biblical truths to their daily life.

 Check for Understanding: This is a short review of what the students learned, to help you assess their progress and what you might need to re-emphasize.

 Memory Verse Activity: This fun activity will help your students memorize the central Bible verse of the lesson.

 Application: This lesson component will challenge your students to apply what they have learned to specific situations in their lives. The application is directly related to the lesson objective.

 Weekly Assignment: Because the purpose of this series is discipleship, the concluding component of the lesson will encourage students to use the lesson application during the week to help them begin developing biblical spiritual habits. At the beginning of the succeeding lesson, the students will discuss how they completed the weekly assignment.

Try to enlist the aid of the parents by explaining about the weekly assignments and what they will do for each child. If possible, explain this when the parents come to drop off or pick up the student, or call them after the first lesson. Some children without a good support system at home may find it difficult to follow through on the weekly assignments. If you have students who do not have support at home, consider meeting with them individually to encourage them and help them grow spiritually. They will also benefit from hearing about other students' experiences. Therefore, make your first activity of the lesson a discussion time about the weekly assignment.

Lesson Structure

The lessons are written to include about an hour's worth of activities. However, you can adapt the material to an hour and fifteen minutes or an hour and a half.

The point of these lesson segments is not to slavishly follow the suggestions given for you. Adapt the lessons to your teaching style without changing the purpose for each component.

The most important aspect of active learning is the debriefing portion of each activity. This debriefing usually involves discussion questions that relate the activity to Scripture and to the lesson objective. Therefore, it is essential to allow enough time during each lesson segment to talk about the activity. If you find that the activities are taking longer than the allotted time, it is better to shorten a later activity than to skip the debriefing questions. If your activities are running short, add questions such as these:

- What will you do differently this week because of what you learned today?

- What feelings did you have during our activity? Why did you have this reaction?

- What was the most important thing you learned? Why was it the most important to you?

- How was the experience of the person in the Bible story like experiences we might have today? How would you have reacted in a similar situation?

As you teach, encourage your students to be risk-takers in what they express. This will require that you treat each person's response with respect. It will also involve listening to what your students say and allowing plenty of time for responses. During this time, assess where your students are spiritually regarding the point of the activity. This discussion will also give you opportunities to talk over many important matters with your students. You may be the only person who can give some students a biblical perspective on life issues. Their responses will help you direct the remainder of the lesson to fit your students' needs.

Most of the debriefing questions are open-ended and require thoughtful answers. Provided after the questions are responses your students are likely to give. If the students' answers seem off-track, help refocus the discussion by restating the question in different words or suggesting a more appropriate response.

The lessons use these conventions to help you follow the lesson structure:

Bold text: instructions to the teacher

Normal text: guided conversation for teaching

- Bulleted questions: questions for classroom discussion

(Italic text in parentheses): possible answers to questions

Gathering Supplies

The Lesson Plan at the beginning of each lesson lists the supplies you will need. Many are items found in typical church classrooms. The lessons assume that the classroom will have a chalkboard and chalk.

Be sure to read and prepare the lesson thoroughly. Some activities may require prior preparation.

Make sure each student has a Bible of his or her own. Encourage students to look up the Bible story as you tell it and to find the memory verse reference. Ask students to read short passages used in the activities, but avoid calling on children to read whose reading skills lag behind others in the group. If you have nonreaders, pair these students with good readers when doing reading activities.

The following rule is essential to keep in mind when teaching children: *The lessons are for the students, not the students for the lessons.* Make sure your students are your priority, not getting through the lesson in a certain way. And have fun learning together!

The Exciting World of the 9- to 12-Year-Old

In some ways, your students live in a world of their own. As teachers, we can never fully understand what they are going through or how they think. But our challenge is to understand them as well as we can and use our knowledge to help them grow mentally, emotionally, socially, physically, and most of all, spiritually. Each child is an individual with unique problems and talents. Each will be at a different place in his or her spiritual journey. At the same time, they will all be affected by similar growing and maturing forces and environments. Keep in mind that their lack of maturity in other areas will affect how they grow spiritually.

If you have previously taught children in this age group, you probably understand how much they are developing in all areas of their lives. The following guidelines will help you see where the student is:

Mental Development
> Moving from literal toward abstract thinking
> Increasing concentration length
> Beginning to understand the significance of past and future but still concerned with the here-and-now
> Creative and curious
> Well-developed problem-solving skills
> Able to think critically

Emotional Development
> Alternating between acting responsibly and childishly
> More self-directed and independent
> Sometimes fears bad situations like parents' divorce or being a victim of violence

Social Development
> Peer-oriented but still looks to adults for guidance
> Relates better with same-sex friends
> Likes having one best friend
> May act in socially inappropriate ways
> Enjoys group activities

Physical Development
> Lots of energy
> Girls may be taller and more coordinated than boys

Likes a variety of activities
Is good with fine motor skills

Spiritual Development
Is developing a value system and a conscience
Can put into practice Bible teachings
Has a clear sense of right and wrong, of fair and unfair
Eager to trust Jesus
Able to make choices and follow through

To help your students build a value system based on God's Word, you will have to move them beyond merely acquiring knowledge to applying biblical truths. The learning process includes these five progressive steps:

1. Feeling

2. Knowing

3. Understanding

4. Applying

5. Practicing

Each lesson is set up to explore your students' feelings about the topic, introduce Bible knowledge, help them apply what they learn, and begin practicing the application on a consistent basis. Each component of the lesson is designed to help move your students through the five progressive steps to making the spiritual concepts part of their lives.

As you teach these lessons, enjoy the world of your students. Do the activities with them. Play the games. Memorize the verse. Enter into the excitement of the activities and the joy of discovering our great and wonderful God. Your journey in discipling children can be just as valuable as theirs will be.

Tips for Teaching Your Students

Each teacher has his or her own style that makes a classroom run well. However, a few basic tips can help you utilize your teaching methods in a more effective manner. The following are suggestions you can use to augment your teaching:

- *Get to know your students.* Every child wants to know that the adults in his life are aware of him and his needs. Begin by calling each student by name. Make a prayer list that includes all your students and keep it up-to-date. Keep track of each student's needs, problems, and talents. Treat each child as an individual.

- *Make your classroom a "safe" zone.* Students at this age can be cruel and thoughtless. Learning skills can be difficult for some students. Other students will have a hard time interacting with children their age. You can help by making sure that each child is treated with respect in your classroom. Praise everyone's accomplishments—even if they do not seem very accomplished to you. Compliment a child who has trouble memorizing when he shows progress. Make a game easier for a child who has poor coordination. And make sure no one in your classroom makes unkind remarks about anyone else. Your "safe" classroom will help students open up during discussion times and feel welcome and comfortable.

- *Look for creative ways to use the available space.* Often we use classroom space the same way all the time. Look around your classroom. Could you move furniture to make the activities work better? Is there space in a fellowship hall, a lobby, or outdoors that would work well for games? Is your classroom big enough to divide into sections for different activities? Can you reserve a corner for discussion and decorate it accordingly?

- *Keep the lesson moving.* Children have a short attention span. They will lose interest if you are not prepared or if you use a slow pace. If students get bored with a game or activity, move on to the debriefing questions.

- *Be aware of your students' moods, personalities, and family situations.* Some days, children will bound into your room talking and ready to go. Other days, it will seem as if you cannot get anyone to respond. An incident during the week may affect a student's behavior. For example, a student whose parents have recently separated may be especially withdrawn or unruly. Learn to recognize the behavior that tells you something is wrong with that child. Keep all your students in prayer for all their needs and concerns.

- *Use consistent discipline with your students.* Write your classroom rules on poster board and post them in your classroom. Then follow the rules. Avoid reprimanding any child in the presence of others. Also, teach your students a signal to get their attention. You might flash the lights on and off or raise your hand for silence. Practice the attention-getting signal until your students obey it. Despite your best efforts, your class will probably have at least one student who will test your patience. As a last resort, you may have to remove an unruly child from the room. Before you begin teaching, work out discipline procedures for unruly students with another adult such as your children's department leader or pastor.

- *Use different teaching styles.* Children, like adults, learn best in different ways. Some are visual learners and learn best when they see things. Others are auditory learners and learn best by hearing. Still others are kinesthetic learners who function best by touching. The lessons are geared to use all types of learning styles, but be aware of how each child learns best so you can help all your students get the most out of the lessons.

- *Be open to adjusting your lesson if the moment warrants.* At times, you will find your students especially open to discussing important topics that the lesson does not cover. Take advantage of these moments to talk with them. Sometimes, an activity will fail to go as planned. When that happens, adjust your debriefing questions to facilitate learning even more. For example, if you were doing an activity with a balloon and the balloon popped before you could finish, you might turn your lesson into an example of how to react when things do not go right.

- *Plan for early arrivers.* Some students will arrive early. Be prepared with activities they can do. One suggestion is to make an ongoing bulletin board that relates to the lesson. For example, Lesson 1 describes the Bible as one of our greatest gifts. Use a gift theme for a bulletin board. On your board, place pieces of wrapping paper and ribbon to look like packages. Underneath each one, put a hidden gift such as a joke or fun saying. In Lesson 4, allow all your students to "open" a gift. Then discuss the kinds of gifts God has given us. Thank God for all He has given us, especially His Word that tells us about His Son.

  You might ask students to arrange chairs, set out supplies, or work on an activity sheet that corresponds with the lesson theme.

  Another idea is to bring picture puzzles that relate to a biblical theme and have students glue them onto large pieces of paper. They can take these puzzles home to remind them that the Bible is a perfect puzzle that will enrich our lives.

- *Use "after class" moments wisely.* Most of your students will be anxious to leave once the lesson is over. Elementary students tend to begin anticipating the next event before the current one ends. But occasionally a student will hang back. Some students enjoy relating to a teacher and may frequently stay behind. Other students may have parents who are involved in other ministries in your church and have been asked to remain in the classroom until they can be picked up. Rather than resenting the extra time children spend in your classroom, plan for these possibilities.

Allow students to help you straighten up the classroom and begin preparing for the next lesson. They could gather supplies, help you photocopy handouts, or do simple cutting preparations. While you work, discuss what they learned during the day's activities.

Use this time to develop a deeper relationship with the students who linger behind. Over the course of a few months, you may end up spending extra time with most of your students. Preteens will open up to you more easily if you talk to them naturally while you are working together on a project. Occasionally, a student may hang back out of a desire to talk about a crisis in his or her life. If necessary, ask for help from the staff in your children's department.

Another "after class" idea is to have students help you plan and put on a reception for their parents. This will help you meet the parents and understand them better. This reception will work well either near the beginning or near the end of the unit. Make sure you send home announcements for the two weeks prior to the reception. Since the event is for the parents, plan simple refreshments that either your children's department can provide or that a few volunteers can supply. Present a Certificate of Completion to each student for completing this Bible study.

God bless you as you reach the newest generation for our Lord Jesus Christ!

What Is the Bible?

BOOK OBJECTIVE	To provide a survey of the Bible.
UNIT OBJECTIVE	To introduce students to the Bible and help them begin to hear, read, study, memorize, and meditate on it regularly.
LESSON 1: Book of Books	*Objective:* To help students learn to recognize the entire Bible as God's revelation of Jesus Christ to us. *Application:* To help students learn the major sections of the Bible.
LESSON 2: Perfect Puzzle	*Objective:* To help students gain confidence in the Bible's authority by looking at the reliability of the Old and New Testaments. *Application:* To help students deal with situations where they need to make God's Word the highest authority.
LESSON 3: Our Treasure	*Objective:* To help students learn how to experience the power of God's Word in their lives. *Application:* To enable students to use a topical Bible study method.
LESSON 4: Book of Wisdom	*Objective:* To help students begin establishing good habits of regular, systematic study of the Bible. *Application:* To enable students to use biographical and chapter Bible study methods.

Have you ever had a time when you thought you knew where you were going but got lost instead? Maybe you were in an unfamiliar area and took a wrong turn. It was late and the sun had gone down. Everything looked different in the dark. As you drove up and down looking for your street, you searched the glove compartment for a map—but you had left it at home. How you wish you had not assumed you knew where you were going!

Now just imagine if you were in this situation and you were only 10 or 11 years old! As a youngster, you have far fewer skills and less knowledge to help you out of your situation. You face greater dangers because of your youth and your small size.

Now imagine how it feels to be that age and open a Bible. Many adults feel overwhelmed when they try to make sense of the Bible. Your students have even less ability to understand the Bible as a complete book and comprehend its blessings in our lives.

For most of their lives, your students have heard bits and pieces of the Bible. They have probably memorized some verses, heard Bible stories, but have never had the advantage of seeing what they have learned put into a historical and theological context. That's why it's so important that your students grasp the basic structure of the Bible and how to study it for themselves.

What God reveals through His Word is a blessing to us. Since the Bible is God's revelation of Himself to man, we know that Christ is God, that He came to earth to die for our sins, and that He arose from the dead and now lives in every believer.

We cannot overemphasize the value of God's Word in daily life. The Scottish pastor and writer Thomas Cuthrie expressed it well:

> The Bible is an armory of heavenly weapons, a laboratory of infallible medicines, a mine of exhaustless wealth. It is a guidebook for every road, a chart for every sea, a medicine for every malady, and a balm for every wound. Rob us of the Bible, and our sky has lost its sun.

The great evangelist D. L. Moody said:

> I prayed for faith, and thought that some day faith would come down and strike me like lightning. But faith did not seem to come. One day I read in the tenth chapter of Romans, "Now faith comes by hearing, and hearing by the Word of God." I had closed my Bible and prayed for faith. I now opened my Bible and began to study, and faith has been growing ever since.

You may be familiar with the book *Mutiny on the Bounty*. Captain Bligh miraculously lived after the mutiny and returned to England to report the crime. Many of the guilty sailors were found and hanged. Several, however, could not be found.

Twenty years passed and the whole incident was forgotten until a ship discovered an uncharted island. When the crew landed, they could hardly believe what they had found: an utter utopia. No disease, no crime, no drunkenness, just grace and harmony.

When the crew learned the reason for the behavior of the islanders, they were amazed. Eight of the Bounty's sailors had fled to this island after the mutiny. They had ravaged the people and all but one of the sailors, Alexander Smith, had died.

In desperation, he had rummaged through all the other men's belongings, looking for more whiskey, when he found a Bible. He read it, believed it, and became a Christian. He introduced the entire population of the island to Christ and they, with him, believed and obeyed the Word of God.

God's Word not only influences men's actions—it transforms men's lives. We need to study the Word of God effectively and carefully interpret it so that we not only possess its truths, but its truths possess us.

As children of God, your students have the Holy Spirit to guide them into all truth as they search the Scriptures. Begin adopting the principles of God's Word through Bible study and then pass on what you learn to your students. Each time you begin a study—either on your own or with your students—ask the Holy Spirit, who inspired holy men of old to record the sacred truths, to make them real in your experiences. Ask the Holy Spirit to help each of you apply what you learn to your daily lives.

The Bible encourages us to memorize Scripture. In Psalm 119:11, the psalmist wrote, "I have hidden your word in my heart that I might not sin against you." Therefore, you and your students will be memorizing verses in each lesson. Encourage your students to keep practicing these verses until they become embedded in their minds. Also remind students to daily read and study the Bible. Any Bible study habits they develop now will absolutely change their lives.

Book of Books

LESSON PLAN

OBJECTIVE: Students will learn to recognize the entire Bible as God's revelation of Jesus Christ to us.

APPLICATION: Students will learn the major sections of the Bible.

LESSON PLAN ELEMENT	ACTIVITY	TIME	SUPPLIES
Opening Activity	*The Greatest Book Ever Given*	7–10	Bible; a box; wrapping paper; bow; tape; 4 or 5 fiction books that have a distinct main character
Bible Story—Assorted Scriptures, Jesus is the central Person of the Bible	*The Central Person of the Bible*	10–15	Bibles; 7 boxes of different sizes (see activity instructions); wrapping paper; 8 slips of paper; pen; tape
Lesson Activity	*What Am I Called?*	7–10	Bibles; pictures of a couch, a dog, a drinking glass, and a baby stroller; paper; pencils
Application	*The Contents*	3–5	Bibles; dry-erase marker or chalk; pencils
Check for Understanding	*A Sword Drill*	7–10	Bibles
Memory Verse Activity	*Picture That!*	3–5	"Picture That!" handout; gift box used in Opening Activity; dry-erase marker or chalk; tape or sticky tack
Weekly Assignment	*Bible Reading Journal*	3–5	Small notebook for each student; pencils

The Bible is God's holy, inspired Word. It is the most powerful and most quoted book in the world. Some of the greatest men in modern history have had a deep respect for the Bible:

Abraham Lincoln: "I believe the Bible is the best gift God has ever given to man. All the good from the Savior of the world is communicated to us through this Book."

Immanuel Kant: "The existence of the Bible, as a book for people, is the greatest benefit which the human race has ever experienced. Every attempt to belittle it is a crime against humanity."

Robert E. Lee: "In all my perplexities and distresses, the Bible has never failed to give me light and strength."

Daniel Webster: "If there is anything in my thoughts or style to commend, the credit is due to my parents for instilling in me an early love of the Scriptures."

Hundreds of millions of people have read its sacred pages, making it the best-selling book of all time.

The composition of the Bible is indeed amazing. A library of sixty-six books, it was written by forty different human authors under the divine inspiration of the Holy Spirit. These writers wrote independently, knowing almost nothing of the others' part. Most had nothing in common, and their literary qualifications were diverse. Moses, for example, was a man of learning, trained in the best universities in Egypt. Peter, on the other hand, was a fisherman without claim to formal education. Yet each man wrote the wisdom of God with powerful force.

It took the Old and New Testament writers fifteen centuries to complete the Bible, which was written in three languages (Hebrew, Aramaic, and Greek) on three continents. Indeed, this collection of books is really one, not sixty-six, for it is coherent in content and progressive truth.

The Bible is composed of 1,189 chapters (929 in the Old Testament and 260 in the New Testament) and utilizes 773,746 words to convey its life-changing message. This literary masterpiece contains history, law, poetry, prophecy, biography, dramatic stories, letters, and revelations. In the words of Sir Isaac Newton, "There are more sure marks of authenticity in the Bible than in any profane [secular] history."

Christian leaders of the fifth century decided upon the list of books to be included in the Bible. This collection of accepted writings came to be known by scholars as the "canon," and were considered inspired and authoritative.

Jesus Christ is the central figure of the Bible. His birth as the Jewish Messiah and Savior of the world was prophesied by Old Testament authors. Their writings contain more than three hundred separate references to the coming of Jesus, with many unique details. Christ fulfilled 100 percent of all the Old Testament predictions of the birth, life, death, and resurrection of the Messiah.

The New Testament makes an even more revolutionary claim: that Jesus Christ is the center of all biblical prophecy. The Scripture proclaims:

> In the past God spoke to our forefathers through the prophets at many times and in various ways, but in these last days he has spoken to us by his Son, whom he appointed heir of all things, and through whom he made the universe (Hebrews 1:1,2).

In the Book of Ephesians, God declares:

> God has told us his secret reason for sending Christ, a plan he decided on in mercy long ago; and this was his purpose: that when the time is ripe he will gather us all together from wherever we are—in heaven or on earth—to be with him in Christ, forever (Ephesians 1:9,10, TLB).

In this lesson and in the next, your students will be discovering the miraculous contents of the Bible. This lesson begins by helping your students understand who the main character is in the Bible—Jesus Christ. In the next lesson, your students will learn how wonderfully the Bible is put together and how it is the final authority for our lives.

As you prepare for the lesson, thank God for all the miraculous truths He has given us and for how He has preserved His Word throughout the centuries. Pass your attitude of thankfulness on to your students.

LESSON PLAN

DING! DONG!

OPENING ACTIVITY: The Greatest Book Ever Given

Before Class: From each fiction book, select a couple of paragraphs that highlight the main character. Use a bookmark to mark each portion you will read. Place the books into a box with the Bible at the bottom. Wrap the box and set the wrapped package in front of the class.

Hold up the gift. Most of us love getting gifts.

- What was the greatest gift you ever received? *(A new bike; video game set; jewelry.)*

- How did you feel when you received that gift? *(So excited I could hardly talk. I was anxious to try out my new gift.)*

When we receive a gift we really want, we are very excited about it at first. We enjoy it everyday. Then sometimes we begin to play with it or use it less because the gift isn't as exciting anymore.

- Has that ever happened to you? Tell us about it. *(Allow students to share times that they have received a great gift and then grown tired of it.)*

Let me show you what I have in my box. **Unwrap the box and pull out the first book. Don't let students see what else is in the box.** It's a book. Many of us have received a book as a gift. Usually, each fiction book has a main character. Let me read a page of this book and see if you can guess who the book is about. **Read a page or two, then let the students guess who or what the main character is. Repeat this procedure with each book until you get to the Bible. Then say:**

The last book I am going to bring out is one that many people have called the greatest book ever written.

- Do you know what book it is? *(The Bible.)*

- What makes the Bible so special? *(Allow volunteers to answer. Use their answers to guide you as you teach this lesson.)*

The greatest gift God ever gave us was His Son, Jesus, who came to die for our sins. The Bible is also one of the greatest gifts God has given us. Without the Bible, we wouldn't know about Jesus and His sacrifice for us. The Bible has many different stories with many different characters. But the Bible still has one main character. Let's find out who this is in our Bible story.

BIBLE STORY: The Central Person of the Bible

 Before Class: Write these references and sentences on separate pieces of paper (include the numbers).

1. OT: Genesis 22:15,17,18—The "offspring" of Abraham refers to Jesus, and all who believe in Jesus are descendants of Abraham.

2. OT: Psalm 22:16–18—Jesus when He was on the cross

3. OT: Isaiah 9:6—Jesus' birth

4. OT: Zechariah 9:9—Jesus when He rode into Jerusalem on a donkey

5. NT: Luke 24:25–27—Jesus explains how the whole Bible is about Him.

6. NT: Acts 3:18—Peter said that the Old Testament was written about Jesus.

7. NT: Revelation 1:1,2—Jesus is in charge of the future.

8. JESUS—The central Person of the Bible and God's gift to us

Find seven boxes of different sizes that can nest inside each other. Begin by putting slip #8 inside the smallest box. Wrap it and tape slip #7 on the wrapping paper. Put it inside the next largest box. Wrap that box and tape slip #6 on the paper. Continue until all boxes are wrapped and all slips of paper are taped onto a box.

Has anyone ever given you a gift that had several parts to it? Perhaps you opened the package to find another package inside. Or maybe someone gave you clues, like in a treasure hunt, where you had to go to several places before you could find the gift.

The Bible is kind of like that. The Bible was given over many years as God gradually told us about His greatest gift. But what was the gift inside that was promised to us by God? We're going to find that out today. We're going to go on a Bible treasure hunt. By the end of our hunt, we'll know what the gift is.

First, let me tell you that the Bible is divided into two parts, the Old Testament and the New Testament. **Open your Bible and show the Old and New Testaments.** This fact is important in understanding about the gift. God gave the Old Testament first. In it, He began to tell us His plan to save sinners. Little by little, God revealed what He would do. Finally, in the New Testament, the central part of God's plan was put into action.

Let's see how God's plan is portrayed in different books of the Bible, from the Old Testament through the New Testament.

Remove the slip taped to the biggest box and have a student read it. Ask a volunteer to look up and read the verse. Make sure your students understand where the verse is located in the Bible so they can understand the progression of verses from the front to the back. Unwrap the biggest box. Take out the smaller wrapped box and have a student read the slip that is taped to the wrapping paper, then have a volunteer read the verse. Continue this process until you have unwrapped the smallest box and read what is on the slip inside.

In the New Testament, God's greatest gift, Jesus, came to earth. The writers of the New Testament wrote about Jesus' life, death, and resurrection. They also wrote about how we are to live as Christians and what is going to happen in the future.

- Why do you think Jesus is the main character in the Bible? *(He is God's Son. He was the only one who could accomplish God's plan to save sinners.)*

- What is the main difference between the Old Testament and the New Testament when we think of Jesus' life? *(He wasn't born in the Old Testament, but God gave clues that He was coming. Everyone knew who Jesus was in the New Testament because He had been born and people knew Him.)*

- What advantages do we have when we read the Bible because we know all about Jesus and His life and death? *(It's easier for us to understand what God was telling about the future in the Old Testament. We know about things that happened just like God said they would happen.)*

The Bible is an amazing book. In the Old Testament, Jesus is called the Messiah, the coming One, the King of kings. In the New Testament, Jesus is called the Savior of the world. The Bible, from beginning to end, is the story of Jesus and what He has done to save us from our sins.

LESSON ACTIVITY: What Am I Called?

Often, we have different names for ordinary things. Let's play a game to see how many you know. **Pass out paper and a pencil to each student.** Number your paper 1 to 5. Leave enough space so that you will be able to write several words under each number. **Hold up the picture of the couch.** Write down what this is called. There are several names for it. List as many different names as you know. **Give students a few minutes to do this. Then ask volunteers to give names it can be called. (Couch; sofa; divan.)**

Hold up the picture of a dog. Write down what this item is called. There are several names for it. List as many different names as you know. **Give them a few minutes to do this. Then ask volunteers to give names it can be called. (Dog; puppy; mutt; mongrel.)**

Hold up the picture of the drinking glass. Write down what this is called. There are several names for it. List as many different names as you know. **Give students a few minutes to do this. Then ask volunteers to give names it can be called. (Cup; glass; tumbler.)**

Hold up the picture of the baby stroller. Write down what this is called. There are several names for it. List as many different names as you know. **Give them a few minutes to do this. Then ask volunteers to give names it can be called. (Stroller; baby carriage; baby buggy; pram.)**

Now think of yourself. What different names do you use? You are probably called by your first name quite a bit. You may be referred to as brother or sister. Your parents may call you son or daughter. In a formal setting you may be called Mr. or Miss. Some of you may have a nickname. Others use their middle name as their designation. Some use their initials.

Allow volunteers to share some unusual names that they are called.

Hold up the Bible. We also have different names for this book. We most often refer to it as the Bible, but the Bible itself never uses that word in any verse. The word *Bible* comes from a Greek word that means a collection of writings or books. Let's look up some verses in the Bible to find some other names given to this book.

Read 1 Corinthians 15:3,4. The Bible is often referred to as the Scriptures. **Read Ephesians 6:17 aloud.**

- What two names are given for the Bible here? *(Sword of the Spirit; Word of God.)*

- What other names have you heard people use to refer to the Bible? *(Holy Bible; the Good Book; God's Word.)*

Just as we have different names for people, animals, and things, the Bible is called by different names. But all the names refer to the same book.

APPLICATION: The Contents

Make sure everyone has a Bible and a pencil. Have students open their Bibles to the Contents page.

Looking at the Contents page is the easiest way to see what is inside a book. We can learn a lot of things about a book this way.

- What are the two main parts of the Bible? *(The Old Testament and the New Testament.)*

Now let's read the first two verses and the last two verses of the Bible. **Have volunteers read Genesis 1:1,2 and Revelation 22:20,21.**

- What time span does the Bible cover? *(From the beginning of creation to when Jesus comes to rule forever.)*

The Bible can also be divided into the kinds of books within each section. Let's look at those. We will start with the Old Testament. **Write the categories and the books on the board as you identify them. Have students follow along and mark the categories on their Bible's Contents page.**

BOOKS OF THE LAW:

Genesis	**Numbers**
Exodus	**Deuteronomy**
Leviticus	

Moses is usually considered the author of the first five books of the Bible. They are books about the early history of humankind.

HISTORICAL BOOKS:

Joshua	1 and 2 Chronicles
Judges	Ezra
Ruth	Nehemiah
1 and 2 Samuel	Esther
1 and 2 Kings	

These next twelve books are the history of God's people, the Israelites. The first six books tell of the beginning of the kingdom, and the next six books tell of the Israelites' punishment by God for their disobedience.

BOOKS OF POETRY:

Job	Ecclesiastes
Psalms	Song of Solomon
Proverbs	

In these books, the writers use beautiful language to tell about God and His wonderful love for us.

MAJOR PROPHETS:

Isaiah	Ezekiel
Jeremiah	Daniel
Lamentations	

These books tell about the coming of the Messiah, Jesus. They were written before Israel was taken into captivity by other nations.

MINOR PROPHETS:

Hosea	Nahum
Joel	Habakkuk
Amos	Zephaniah
Obadiah	Haggai
Jonah	Zechariah
Micah	Malachi

These books are called Minor Prophets only because they are shorter than the Major Prophets, not because they are less important. They also give prophecies about the coming Messiah, Jesus.

Now we turn to the New Testament.

GOSPELS:

Matthew	Luke
Mark	John

The New Testament begins with the story of Jesus. The first four books tell of His birth, life, death, and resurrection.

HISTORY OF THE EARLY CHURCH:

Acts

This book gives the exciting stories of how Paul and the apostles started the Christian church.

PAULINE EPISTLES AND HEBREWS:

Romans	**1 and 2 Thessalonians**
1 and 2 Corinthians	**1 and 2 Timothy**
Galatians	**Titus**
Ephesians	**Philemon**
Philippians	**Hebrews**
Colossians	

These thirteen books are letters to churches. (The word "epistles" means "letters.") Most were written by Paul and were named for the church or person to which Paul sent the letter. No one knows for sure who wrote the Book of Hebrews, but many people think Paul wrote that too.

GENERAL EPISTLES:

James	**1, 2, and 3 John**
1 and 2 Peter	**Jude**

These seven books were written by authors other than Paul. The name of the book is the name of the author.

REVELATION:

Revelation

This is the only book in the New Testament that is full of prophecies. It describes the end times and the glory of Jesus Christ when He comes again to reign forever.

Read Revelation 22:18,19.

- What warning does God give to us in these verses? *(We shouldn't add or take away anything from the Bible.)*

- What new things have you learned about the Bible that change the way you think about it? *(Allow students to respond freely.)*

One way we can learn how to use the Bible in a better way is to memorize the books of the Bible in order. That way, when we need to look up a verse, we can find it easier. We will begin doing that in our Weekly Assignment.

CHECK FOR UNDERSTANDING: A Sword Drill
Divide students into two teams.

You have learned that the Bible is divided into two parts.

- What is the first part called? *(Old Testament.)*

- What is the second part called? *(New Testament.)*

You also became familiar with the sixty-six books of the Bible by looking at the Contents page. To see how familiar you have become with the books of the Bible, we are going to have a "Sword Drill." If you remember, the Bible can be referred to as the "Sword of the Spirit." This is where the name "Sword Drill" comes from.

To play, hold your Bibles closed. I will call out a book of the Bible, and will repeat the name of the book. Then I will say "go." When you have found that book in your Bible, stand up. After I say "stop," no other people can stand up. Each person standing will receive a point for his or her team.

Name several books of the Bible, using this list or making up your own. It is best to start with easier books. Say "go," wait one minute, then say "stop." (Adjust the amount of time according to how many students find the book within that time.)

Genesis	1 Kings
Revelation	Job
Matthew	Ephesians
Psalms	1 Peter
John	Ruth
Exodus	Luke
Acts	Malachi

MEMORY VERSE ACTIVITY: Picture That!

      12   1   2   3   4

2 Timothy 3:16,17— "[All Scripture] [is God-breathed] [and is useful for] [teaching,]

    5   6   7   8   9

[rebuking,] [correcting] [and training] [in righteousness,] [so that the man of God]

      10   11

[may be thoroughly equipped] [for every good work.]

Before Class: Make a copy of the "Picture That!" master, enlarging it if possible. Cut apart the illustrations. Write the memory verse on the board. Using tape or sticky tack, place each picture above the word section to which it belongs (use the corresponding numbers above the verse as a guide.)

Read 2 Timothy 3:16,17 as a class. This is an important verse for us. It tells us many things about the Bible. We must know that all Scripture is God-breathed. God-breathed means that God spoke to each of the writers of the individual books, and they wrote down exactly what He said. The Bible teaches us, shows us what we are doing wrong, and trains us to do what is right. The Bible helps us in all the works of good service we do for others and God. Let's read the verse a couple more times together. Look at the word pictures to help you remember each part. **You may want to point to each picture as the students say the words so that they connect each section with the picture. Then give each word picture to a volunteer. Ask volunteers to line up and say the words that go with their pictures. (If you have fewer than twelve students, give some students two consecutive pictures.)**

Then divide the class into two teams. Put the word pictures upside down in the gift box. Erase the verse on the board. Have teams take turns selecting a picture from the box and placing it on the board. As each part is placed correctly, that team will get a point, for a total of twelve points per game. Other team members are not allowed to give hints. Do this several times. Then put the picture parts in order on the board, and ask individuals to repeat the verse to you.

WEEKLY ASSIGNMENT: Bible Reading Journal

Teaching Tip: During the thirteen lessons in this study, you will be instructed to help your students memorize the books of the Bible. If your students have already learned these Bible facts, omit this activity and concentrate on the other activities. Use the Bible Journal throughout this series to help your students develop a habit of regular Bible reading.

To help us "navigate" or get around the Bible easily, we will be memorizing the books of the Bible in order. **Pass out small notebooks and pencils, and have students write their names on the front of their notebooks. Have them write "Books of the Law" on page one, along with the first five books of the Old Testament: Genesis, Exodus, Leviticus, Numbers, and Deuteronomy. Instruct students to memorize the names of these books this week.**

Another way we can learn more about the Bible is to keep reading it. Some people read through the entire Bible every year. That is a good goal for when you are an adult. But for right now, you can start developing the habit of reading the Bible every day. Let's do this by creating a Bible Reading Journal.

On page two of your journal, write these reading assignments:

Day 1—Genesis 1
Day 2—Genesis 2
Day 3—Genesis 3
Day 4—Genesis 4
Day 5—Genesis 6
Day 6—Genesis 7
Day 7—Genesis 8

Give students time to write. Notice that we skipped Genesis chapter 5. In our daily reading, we'll just be reading selected chapters. After you read each passage, put a checkmark beside it. Bring your Bible Reading Journals to our next class.

Close in prayer, thanking God for the Bible and all the wisdom it teaches us.

Picture That!

1.

2.

3.

4.

5.

6.

7.

8.

9.

10.

11.

2 Timothy 3:16,17

12.

Perfect Puzzle

LESSON PLAN

OBJECTIVE: Students will gain confidence in the Bible's authority by looking at the reliability of the Old and New Testaments.

APPLICATION: Students will begin dealing with situations where they need to make God's Word the highest authority.

LESSON PLAN ELEMENT	ACTIVITY	TIME	SUPPLIES
Opening Activity	*Puzzling Pieces*	7–10	Paper; pencils; 100- to 500-piece puzzle with box
Bible Story—Assorted Scriptures, overview of the Bible	*A Story in Parts*	10–15	Bible; 1 copy of "A Story in Parts"; scissors
Lesson Activity	*Who Said So?*	7–10	Bibles; 3 pieces of paper; 3 pencils
Check for Understanding	*Awesome Authorities*	3–5	Bibles; slips of paper; pencils
Memory Verse Activity	*Puzzling Over a Verse*	7–10	2 posterboards of different colors; dry-erase marker or chalk; masking tape
Application	*The Highest Authority*	3–5	"Bible Puzzle" handouts
Weekly Assignment	*Bible Puzzle*	3–5	Scissors; envelopes; pencils; "Bible Puzzle" handouts

Belief in the absolute authority of the Scriptures is foundational to our faith. God has given us many assurances that the Bible is truly God's Word. The authenticity of the Old Testament has been validated even more in the last few years with archaeological finds and other proofs. Researchers in Israel subjected the first five books of the Old Testament to exhaustive computer analysis. They came to a different conclusion than they expected.

Skeptics had long assumed that the Torah, or Books of Moses, was the work of multiple authors. But Scripture scholar Moshe Katz and computer expert Menachem Wiener of the Israel Institute of Technology refuted this belief.

The material, they concluded, suggests a single, inspired author—in fact, it could not have been put together by human capabilities at all. "So we need a nonrational explanation," he said. "And ours is that the Torah was written by God through the hand of Moses."

The Old Testament was considered by its writers to be the inspired and authoritative Word of God (Moses: Exodus 24:4; David: 2 Samuel 23:2; Jeremiah: Jeremiah 1:4).

Our Lord Himself, the New Testament writers, and the early church also affirmed its authenticity. Jesus frequently referred to Old Testament Scriptures during His earthly ministry (John 10:35; Luke 24:44,45). He also quoted Scripture numerous times (Mark 12:35,36; Luke 4:4,8,12). Many other passages testify to the authority of the Old Testament, often with the words, "that the scripture might be fulfilled" (John 19:24,36). As the early church grew, the church fathers were unanimous about one thing: the entire Old Testament was given by the Holy Spirit through men.

Christianity began with the preaching of Jesus but was spread word-of-mouth by the faithful witness of His followers. Eventually, the oral gospel and the writings of the apostles to the churches were preserved for us in the books of the New Testament.

These twenty-seven books represent only a few of the numerous writings produced by early Christians, many of whom attempted to reinterpret the sayings and teachings of Christ. For more than two hundred years, the church fathers could not decide which of those works should be considered as having been written under the guidance and inspiration of the Holy Spirit. The need for unity in belief and practice among Christians eventually led the fathers to separate the writings that were in harmony with the teachings of Jesus from those that were not.

The authoritative list of books developed slowly and gradually under the influence of the Holy Spirit. By the year A.D. 400 most Christians had accepted the twenty-seven books that now compose our New Testament.

As you prepare for this lesson, pick up your Bible and thumb through the pages. Have you ever thought about its origin and how its sixty-six books were collected into one volume? Have you ever considered how the precise fulfillment of the immense body of biblical prophecy is found in one unique and revolutionary man—Jesus of Nazareth? Claiming that He was the predicted One of old, Jesus stepped into time. And the pieces of the prophetic puzzle slipped into place. In this lesson, your students will learn about the miraculous authority of our Bible and gain confidence in its power to change and direct their lives.

LESSON PLAN

DING! DONG!

OPENING ACTIVITY: Puzzling Pieces

Have your students report on what they learned through their Bible reading. If desired, review their Bible Reading Journals to see how consistently the students are reading their Bibles. Review the names of the Books of the Law.

Keep the picture on the puzzle box covered. Pass out paper, pencil, and a puzzle piece to each student. Try to select pieces that are very different in color.

Look at your puzzle piece. What is shown on your piece? Try to decide what the entire puzzle picture is by looking at your piece. When you have come up with your idea, place your puzzle piece on your paper where you think the piece would fit in the puzzle. Trace around your puzzle piece. Then draw the puzzle picture as you imagine it. Your drawing does not have to be good or fancy. Do not talk to your neighbor or look at your neighbor's paper.

Give students time to think and draw. When they finish, have students tell what they envisioned the picture to look like. If they would like, let them show their drawings too.

Show the front of the puzzle box.

It is very hard to identify a picture based on just one small part. We need all the pieces to help us really know what the picture is.

- How was your idea of the picture different from what it really was? *(Allow students to respond.)*

- Would it have helped to have seen more pieces of the puzzle? Why? *(I would get more clues to what was on the picture. I could try to put some pieces together to help me.)*

For us humans, the Bible is like a puzzle, too. It's hard for us to understand how all the stories, teachings, and commands fit together. Just imagine how hard it must have been for the writers to write the Bible without having the full story as we do. Just imagine what the writer of Genesis, the first book in the Bible, might have been thinking when he wrote. He did not know about David or Solomon or the prophets or Jesus. But at the same time, I am sure he was excited about the things he was writing about God.

As we learned in our previous lesson, the Bible is divided into many parts. In fact, we learned that the Bible's two main parts, the Old and the New Testaments, are split into sixty-six books. Think of how many different people are mentioned in the Bible. **Allow students to quickly mention lots of Bible characters. Add some of your own.**

Think of how many different places are mentioned in the Bible. **Allow students to mention as many places as they can think of. Add other places such as Egypt, Canaan, Rome, Greece, Ephesus, the Jordan River, the Sea of Galilee, etc.**

In our Bible story, we will do an activity that shows how marvelously the Bible is put together.

BIBLE STORY: A Story in Parts

Cut apart the five story parts on the "A Story in Parts" reproducible page. Divide students into five groups and give each group one part. As a group, read over your story. I will give you a few minutes to plan how to act it out. Have a good reader in your group be the narrator to read your story as you act it out.

Give students time to plan their actions. Then have each group act out their story in order of the number on their slip. Gather groups for discussion.

You did well in your acting. They were interesting stories.

- When you were brainstorming with your group, did you figure out that your group's story was really part of a complete story with several parts? Why or why not? *(No, because I didn't know what the other stories were about. Yes, I just suspected it was.)*

- How did the stories all fit together to make one story? *(They all had the same main character even though he wasn't called by the same name in each one. The story was all about one long journey.)*

This is similar to the way the Bible is put together. Many different writers all wrote at different times. The Book of Genesis tells about the beginning of time, the creation. **Read Genesis 1:1.** The Book of Jonah is about a prophet who lived before Jesus. The Lord ordered him to preach to the people of Nineveh. **Read Jonah 1:1.** The Book of Mark is about the life of Jesus. **Read Mark 1:1.** The Book of 1 Corinthians is a letter to one of the first Christian churches. **Read 1 Corinthians 1:2.** The Book of Revelation gives the story of the future of the earth when Jesus comes to rule forever. **Read Revelation 1:1.** Some of these writings seem like separate stories. But when all the writings or books in the Bible are put together, the Bible is about the same Person, Jesus. We learned this in our last lesson. All the books of the Bible also fit together by the sense they make.

Ask the following questions, bringing out the points in italics after the question.

- How is Part 1 of our story like the story of the Bible? *(Jesus went on a journey to earth, but He had not yet been crowned King of the universe.)*

- How is Part 2 like the story of the Bible? *(Jesus came to find His lost lambs—people who don't know God.)*

- How is Part 3 like the story of the Bible? *(Jesus fights our enemies, Satan and all his forces, and always wins.)*

- How is Part 4 like the story of the Bible? *(Jesus shares all He has and all His love with us, especially during our times of trouble.)*

- How is Part 5 like the story of the Bible? *(Jesus is the only One worthy to be crowned the King of the universe. And He will be!)*

One good way we can know that the Bible is true is because it all fits together. It is the Perfect Puzzle. Even the writers of the Bible didn't understand how the story was going to fit together. They just wrote what God told them to write.

There are several other ways we can know that the Bible is absolutely true. We'll find out about that in our Lesson Activity.

LESSON ACTIVITY: Who Said So?

We often do things under the authority of others. In school you often ask the question, "Did the teacher say we could?" At home you might tell your friends, "I can sleep over at your house. My parents say it is OK." During a traffic jam, you are allowed to pass through an intersection when the traffic officer motions you through. Let's play a game of "Solomon Says, Simon Says" to help us understand authority. Solomon is wise. Simon is foolish. I am going to give you a series of commands. Obey only the commands that Solomon says. He is the final authority. Do not obey the commands that Simon says. He is not an authority.

Have everyone stand. Give the following commands or others of your choice. Intersperse the "Simon says" commands and "Solomon says" commands. For example, "Simon says, 'Touch your head.'" Or "Solomon says, 'Clap your hands.'" If someone acts out a "Simon says" command, he or she must sit down. Do the commands quickly to confuse the students. Use the following ideas or ones of your own.

Touch your head	Clap your hands
Lift one leg	Hop on one foot
Jump up	Touch the floor
Wave	Close your eyes
Run in place	Touch your nose
Touch your elbow	Spin around

When most of the students are seated, say: It is easy to get tricked into listening to the wrong authority. That is why it is important for us to believe in the authority of the Bible. We should know and believe that it contains God's inspired words so we know what we are supposed to do. Let's break into three groups and look up verses in the Bible. These verses, from three different sources, give testimony that the Bible is God's Word. You should be able to give a short report on what you find. **Divide students into three groups. Pass out a piece of paper and a pencil to each group for notes. Assign each group one of the following sets of verses. Give groups time to write a report on what the verses say about the authority of the Bible.**

TESTIMONY OF THE WRITERS:

2 Samuel 23:2

Isaiah 8:1,5

Exodus 32:16

TESTIMONY OF JESUS:

Matthew 4:4,7,10

Matthew 5:17,18

Matthew 22:29–32

TESTIMONY OF THE APOSTLES:

> Romans 3:2
> 1 Corinthians 11:23
> 2 Timothy 3:16

After a few minutes, have groups give their reports. When the students have finished their reports, say: The writers of the Bible books, Jesus, and the apostles all gave testimony that the Bible is God's Word. This should help us know that the Bible is true.

CHECK FOR UNDERSTANDING: Awesome Authorities

With the students in the same three groups, hand each person three slips of paper and a pencil. Have students label the slips "the writers," "Jesus," and "the apostles." You have learned that there were three authorities who say that the Bible is God's inspired Word. They help us know that the Bible is true and comes directly from God. I am going to read a verse from the Bible. I want you to decide which authority is speaking. Hold up the correct answer when you know it.

Read the following verses and have students lift up one slip of paper with the correct answer for each verse.

Revelation 1:1: *The Apostles (John)*

John 5:39: *Jesus*

Jeremiah 1:9: *The Writers (Jeremiah)*

2 Samuel 23:2: *The Writers (David)*

2 Peter 1:21: *The Apostles (Peter)*

Matthew 5:17,18: *Jesus*

These three authorities help us know that the Bible is truly God's inspired Word.

MEMORY VERSE ACTIVITY: Puzzling Over a Verse

Matthew 24:35—"Heaven and earth will pass away, but my words will never pass away."

> *Before Class:* Print the words of the memory verse on posterboard. Cut into puzzle pieces. Make a matching set with a different color of posterboard. Write the memory verse on the board.

Have your students read the memory verse together. Our verse today is talking about God's Word, the Bible. No matter what happens in our world, we can know that God's Word will always be here.

Have the students recite the verses several more times, then erase it from the board. One at a time, have students choose a colored puzzle piece and assemble puzzles on the

floor until both puzzles are complete. Say the verse together.

Divide the class into two teams. Scatter the pieces of both sets of the memory-verse puzzle on one side of the room face down. Mark a starting point on the other side of the room with masking tape.

We are going to play the "Verse Puzzle" game. You will be competing against the other team. Your goal is to be the first team to assemble your puzzle and recite the verse together.

Line up students behind the starting point. Assign each team a puzzle color. When you say "go," a member of each team goes to the scattered puzzle pieces, picks one up, and brings it back to where the teams will build their puzzles. As soon as the piece is fit into place, the next person on the team goes to pick up a piece. The winning team is the one that completes its puzzle first and recites the verse correctly. To add to the fun, you could have students walk, hop, skip, etc., to reach the puzzle pieces. Play the game several times, then have individuals say the verse to you if you choose.

APPLICATION: The Highest Authority

So far, we have learned that we can rely on and trust in the Bible. The Bible has been proved to be true. We know this fact for sure because:

- The Bible is miraculously one story told in many books by many writers.

- The writers of the Bible said that God (through the Holy Spirit) gave them the words of the Bible to write down.

- Jesus taught that the Scriptures are from God.

- The apostles told us that the Old and New Testaments are the perfect words of God.

What will you do when you get in a situation where you need to trust what the Bible says? If we decide right now to rely on the Bible rather than the words of people or our own negative thoughts, our decision will help us to make the Bible our authority when problems come up later.

I'm going to read you a situation. Then let's discuss how you would handle the problem by relying on God's Word. We will learn some principles as we discuss them. **Give the following situations. Ask the questions, allowing students to respond freely, but making sure you conclude with the italicized answers.**

1. God's Word is a higher authority than any person.

   You are in school one day and your teacher begins a science lesson. He brings up the subject of evolution. He says, "Scientists tell us that nothing on earth was created. Instead, everything we see around us—plants, animals, rocks, stars—came from a single atom many billions and billions of years ago."

- As Christians, how are we to treat our teachers? (*God says we must always treat authorities with respect.*)

- What is wrong with what the teacher is teaching? *(He is saying that God did not create anything, that there is no God.)*

- What does the Bible teach about this? *(Many verses throughout the Bible say that God created everything.)*

- Who has the higher authority, God or the teacher? *(God.)*

- How could you handle this situation in a good way? *(I could tell my teacher that I disagree with what he says and tell him that I believe God created everything. But I must say this very respectfully.)*

2. God's Word is a higher authority than any of my feelings.

   You belong to a group of close friends in your class. You have lots of fun together after school. Since you all live in the same neighborhood, you all ride your bikes home together. But one of your friends starts bugging the rest of you by laughing too much and talking too loudly and saying dumb things. Some of your other friends get together and plan to flatten the tires of that person's bike. You agree with the plan because you don't want that person to ride home with the group either. And it only seems fair since that person is so obnoxious.

- As Christians, how are we to treat other people? *(With kindness and love.)*

- What was wrong with the feelings you had about the obnoxious person? *(They are not how a Christian is supposed to treat others.)*

Read Ephesians 4:32.

- How can you use this verse to overcome wrong feelings in this kind of situation? *(God tells us to be kind to one another.)*

- Who has the higher authority, God's Word or your feelings? *(God's Word.)*

- How could you handle this situation? *(I could refuse to agree to do something mean to that friend and tell my other friends good things about that person.)*

Pass out "Bible Puzzle" handouts.

All of us sometimes have doubts about God and the Bible. That's because we're human, and we can't always control our feelings. The three verses printed on the Bible Puzzle can help you when you have any doubts about how trustworthy the Bible is.

Have volunteers read the verses.

We should spread the news about the authority of the Bible. Everyone needs to obey and trust God's Word. In our Weekly Assignment, we'll learn a way we can do this.

WEEKLY ASSIGNMENT: Bible Puzzle

Teaching Tip: If you have time, have students glue their "Bible Puzzles" to a piece of heavier colored paper or posterboard before cutting out the Bible shape and the individual pieces.

This week the students will begin memorizing the names of the twelve Historical Books. Instruct students to list these books in their Bible Reading Journal following the list of the Books of the Law. Have them write the heading "Historical Books" followed by the book names: Joshua, Judges, Ruth, 1 and 2 Samuel, 1 and 2 Kings, 1 and 2 Chronicles, Ezra, Nehemiah, Esther. Have students write their reading assignment for the week in their Bible Reading Journal:

Day 1—Joshua 1
Day 2—Joshua 2
Day 3—Joshua 3
Day 4—Joshua 4
Day 5—Joshua 6
Day 6—Joshua 23
Day 7—Joshua 24

Pass out scissors and envelopes. Make sure students have pencils and their "Bible Puzzle" handouts. Instruct students to cut apart the puzzle pieces. Have them write "Bible Puzzle" on the envelope and put the puzzle pieces inside.

This week, explain to at least two people how reliable the Bible is. To do this, read the sentence and Bible verse on each puzzle piece to that person, then put the pieces in place to complete the puzzle. You may want to keep the completed puzzle near your Bible where you have your quiet time with God each day.

Close by thanking God for His miraculous, perfect Word, the Bible.

A Story in Parts

1 Once there was a Prince who planned to make a long journey. He lived in a kingdom ruled by his father, the old King. But the kingdom had been missing something for many, many years, something important—its crown. In the crown was the kingdom's wealth in jewels: emeralds, rubies, sapphires, and the biggest diamond anyone had ever seen. The Prince's father was going to step down from his throne. But he needed the crown to turn the kingdom over to his son, the Prince.

Before the Prince started his journey to search for the crown, he consulted with all the wise men of the land. None of them knew where he should go or who might have the crown. So the Prince packed his bag with some items: a staff, a sword, and a loaf of bread.

Early in the morning, he got up, put on his warmest cloak, saddled his magnificent horse, and rode out of the palace. The huge white palace walls sparkled in the dawn. Without looking back, he clopped across the bridge over the moat and set off toward the rising sun. Soon, he disappeared over the lush green hills of the kingdom.

2 A lonely horseman pulled on the reins as his huge white horse stumbled in the darkness and almost fell over the vicious vines tangled around the tree trunks. The forest he was in was so thick that the sunlight never passed through the leaves to hit the ground. The air smelled damp and moldy.

After traveling for long hours in the eerie woods, the horse suddenly stumbled over something white laying on the forest floor. The vines had almost covered it, but it moved slightly.

The rider knew that if he dismounted from his horse, he too would be hopelessly snarled in the vines. For a moment, he considered what to do.

Then he reached back into his bag bundled on the back of his horse and took out a long stick with a curved end. He began whacking away at the vines, beating them off the small figure. Soon, he loosened the vines enough so the small white animal could raise its head. It was a little lost lamb. Quickly, the horseman pulled off more vines until the lamb was free. Then he reached down with the curved end of the stick and lifted up the trembling animal. He cradled the lamb in his arm until it stopped shaking. Then he urged his horse onward until he could break free from the forest to the gentle pastureland beyond.

3 Both the man in ragged clothes and his horse were tired and thin from their long journey. As they came over the rocky hill, he saw a small farmhouse in a valley. The house was surrounded by a dozen knights in dark armor. They were attacking the farmhouse.

The screams of children could be heard from inside the house as the knights ran a battering ram into the front door.

The ragged rider took one look at the scene and a new energy came into him. He whipped out his shiny sword. As he held it up, it seemed as if electricity flowed from his arm into the sword until the metal glowed. No one could doubt that he was a valiant Knight.

With a bloodcurdling yell, he charged down into the valley, riding around the huge rocks and through the fields straight at the warriors. When they saw him coming, their faces filled with fear. They turned to fight him, but they were no match for his glowing sword. Within minutes, they were fleeing in the opposite direction, blood flowing from many wounds.

The door to the farmhouse flew open and a joyful mother, father, and four little children stumbled out to meet the ragged Knight. He dismounted and they hugged him and invited him to share in their supper of porridge.

After spending the night in the small cottage, the Knight rode off toward the sea.

4 The passenger huddled deeper into his cloak as the fierce waves crashed harder against the ship. The creaking masts were bare, with no sails to save the ship. Sailors ran across the deck, throwing cargo overboard to lighten the ship. The clouds swirled so darkly that the day seemed like night.

Below deck, horses kicked and neighed in fear. The passenger thought of his brave white steed among them. He also thought of his only belongings, a bag tucked safely away below deck.

A huge wave crashed over the deck, soaking everything in sight—the sailors, the passenger, and the few barrels left onboard. The sailors hung on for their lives.

As if that ferocious wave was its last huge breath, the storm began to die. A weak sun peeked through the racing clouds.

The men went into the ship's cabin to find something to eat. The cook brought out the last remaining barrel of food, soaked by seawater. The men tried to chew the ruined food.

Seeing this, the passenger quietly slipped out of the cabin and made his way down below deck. He grabbed his bag and returned to the cabin. He opened the bag and took out a brown, soft loaf of bread. The smell of the bread wafted around the table. He passed it around and each sailor pulled off a large chunk and gratefully ate.

The ship sailed toward the sandy shores now visible on the horizon.

5 The young Prince was mounted on his magnificent stallion. His head was bare, but his shoulders were draped with a rich purple robe. He rode along the gently lapping waves of a sugar-white beach.

Thousands of people had gathered to cheer him. They had heard of his reputation even these many thousands of miles from his palace. They had heard of his exploits—his gentleness in the darkest places, his fearlessness in battling enemies, his bravery in the face of natural forces, his loving generosity.

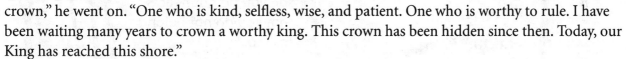

Suddenly, the crowd parted and an old man dressed in a thin brown robe walked toward the King. The King pulled up on his horse and dismounted. He stood humbly before the old man.

"I have been looking for a person," the old man said. "For someone who is worthy to wear this crown." He held out a sparkling, gem-filled crown. "Only one person can wear this crown," he went on. "One who is kind, selfless, wise, and patient. One who is worthy to rule. I have been waiting many years to crown a worthy king. This crown has been hidden since then. Today, our King has reached this shore."

With that, the old man placed the crown on the young King's head. It fit perfectly. Thousands of cheers rang along the shore and the sun seemed to shine with a new brightness.

The King had been crowned!

Bible Puzzle

The Bible is reliable. We can trust the authority of the Bible because:

We listen to the writers of the Bible who wrote the words of God!

John 8:47: "He who belongs to God hears what God says. The reason you do not hear is that you do not belong to God."

We listen to the words of Jesus!

John 18:37: "You are right in saying I am a king. In fact, for this reason I was born, and for this I came into the world, to testify to the truth. Everyone on the side of truth listens to me."

We listen to the words of the apostles who saw Jesus!

1 John 4:6: "We are from God, and whoever knows God listens to us; but whoever is not from God does not listen to us. This is how we recognize the Spirit of truth and the spirit of falsehood."

Our Treasure

LESSON PLAN

OBJECTIVE: Students will learn how to experience the power of God's Word in their lives.

APPLICATION: Students will use a topical Bible study method.

LESSON PLAN ELEMENT	ACTIVITY	TIME	SUPPLIES
Opening Activity	*Powerful Puffs*	5–7	3 heavy books per group; 1 large food-storage bag per group
Bible Story—2 Kings 22:1–23:25, King Josiah finds the Book of the Law in the temple	*The Lost Treasure*	10–15	Bibles; scroll, robe, and crown (optional)
Lesson Activity	*The Bible Changes Our Lives*	7–10	Bibles; paper; pencils; dry-erase marker or chalk
Application	*A Topical Study on Truth*	7–10	"To Tell the Truth" handouts; pencils; topical Bible, concordance, and Bible dictionary (if available); Bibles with concordances
Check for Understanding	*Initial It*	3–5	Dry-erase markers or chalk
Memory Verse Activity	*It's in the Bag*	5–8	2 bags from Opening Activity; yellow construction paper; scissors; fine-point marker
Weekly Assignment	*What's the Truth?*	3–5	"To Tell the Truth" handouts; Bibles with concordances (to lend out if possible)

Lila and her husband were expecting their fourth child and were looking forward to the new baby's arrival with eager anticipation. Then, unexpectedly, their dreams were shattered by a miscarriage.

Not only was Lila grieved by the loss of the child, it soon became apparent that her life was in grave danger. Serious complications suddenly became evident, and she was rushed by ambulance to the hospital.

Lila was vaguely aware of her surroundings as she slipped in and out of consciousness. Her family was at her side encouraging her, and many friends and loved ones were praying fervently.

During the crisis, she found it nearly impossible to focus her mind on anything except for one clear expression that persisted in her mind. "I can endure . . . I can survive . . . I can withstand . . . all things through Christ who strengthens me."

Somehow, despite the loss of blood and the close proximity of death, she was aware that she was not remembering the words just right. Yet she intuitively understood that God was promising to see her through.

Two weeks later, she returned home weakened but alive. While reading her Bible, she suddenly remembered the exact Scripture: "I can do all things through Christ who strengthens me" (Philippians 4:13, NKJ).

How she praised God for His Word, which had penetrated the fog of unconsciousness with a powerful promise of strength and provision!

In the Epistle to Hebrews, we read:

> The word of God is living and active. Sharper than any double-edged sword, it penetrates even to dividing soul and spirit, joints and marrow; it judges the thoughts and attitudes of the heart (Hebrews 4:12).

God's holy, inspired Word has several characteristics that guarantee powerful results.

First, *it is infused with the Holy Spirit*. It has been said that a Bible that is falling apart usually belongs to a person who isn't. That is because God's Word is energetic and active, speaking to today's world and our own personal needs and circumstances.

Second, *God's Word is truth*. It awakens our conscience. With the power to reach into the private corners of our hearts, the Word bares our motives and secret feelings and reveals our hidden longings.

Third, *God's Word discerns our true character*. It exposes the weaknesses in our attitudes and conduct, enabling us to correct ourselves by the power of His Holy Spirit.

As you prepare for this lesson, I urge you to be engaged in a daily practice of hiding the Word of God in your heart, drawing upon its wisdom for your life. Remember that whatever you learn in your search through God's Word will be an advantage to your students. Keep a Bible Reading Journal along with them, memorize the books of the Bible if you haven't already done so, and study God's Word each week. It will enrich your time together in class and help you truly experience the power of God's Word in your life. Also familiarize yourself with various Bible study tools. The lesson refers to these: topical Bible (arranged by topical studies); concordance (index of all the words in the Bible); Bible dictionary (explains biblical terms).

LESSON PLAN

OPENING ACTIVITY: Powerful Puffs

 Before Class: Set out books and bags at three or four work areas.

Review the names of the Historical Books. Then ask your students about what they read in their Bible Reading Journals since the last session.

Let students describe how they used their "Bible Puzzles." Discuss how people reacted when they were told about the reliability of the Bible.

How do you determine what is weak and what is strong? Sometimes we think power comes only from large machines or from big people with bulging muscles. Let's see how powerful air and a plastic bag can be.

Divide students into groups of three or four and send them to the work areas.

 Teaching Tip: For health reasons, make sure that only one person blows into each bag.

Let's see if the air in a bag can lift one book. Set one of your books on top of the bag and blow into it. **Give groups time to do this. As the bag fills with air, the book will be lifted up.**

Now let's try this with two books. **Allow each group time to add a second book on top of the first and blow into the bag.** Finally, let's try three books. **Allow groups time to do this.**

Most of us don't think of air as very powerful. But it can be. Think of the vehicles that brought you here today. They weigh thousands of pounds, yet they are held up by the air in the tires. Air can be very powerful.

Hold up your Bible. This Bible is very small and many people think it's powerless. Yet it contains the greatest power we will ever know. **Read Hebrews 4:12.** This verse tells us that the Word of God is more powerful than a double-edged sword. A double-edged sword is sharp on both sides. It can cut whichever way you hold it and swing it. It is a very effective weapon. What this verse is saying is that the Bible can penetrate or cut into our very souls, thoughts, and attitudes. It can make big changes in our life. What would happen if we didn't have the Word of God? What if it was lost and no one had a copy? This very thing happened long ago. Let's listen to a Bible story about this.

BIBLE STORY: The Lost Treasure

Select three readers to play the part of the narrator, Hilkiah, and King Josiah. Give each reader a Bible with the appropriate verses marked or a slip of paper with the Bible verses

written on it. Open your Bible and tell the following story from 2 Kings 22:1—23:25.

Optional Activity: Bring a scroll (on which you've written the verses) for the narrator to read from. Bring a robe for Hilkiah the priest to wear and a crown for King Josiah.

Can you imagine what your life would be like if you had never seen a Bible, never heard it read, and didn't even know what God had said in His Word? It would be like losing the greatest treasure you had ever known. That happened to some people long ago.

The Israelites, who were God's people, had turned their backs on Him and disobeyed Him. They were worshiping horrible idols, even taking their idol worship into God's holy temple. They were ruled by several wicked kings in a row who did not tell them about God and who behaved very wickedly. Children grew up not knowing anything about God, His promises, and His warnings about sinful behavior. In fact, the Word of God was a lost treasure. No one knew where it was.

Then a new king came to power. He was only eight years old when he was crowned. His name was Josiah. **Have the narrator read the verse:** "He did what was right in the eyes of the LORD and walked in all the ways of his father David, not turning aside to the right or to the left" (2 Kings 22:2). This means that he followed his great, great, great grandfather David's godly example.

But the people had not followed God in such a long time that they didn't really know how to obey God. So the first thing Josiah ordered was that all idols and other bad things be removed from God's temple. The priests were responsible for that job.

The king's secretary, who was named Shaphan, was responsible for bringing the money to the priests so they could repair the temple. One day, Hilkiah, the high priest, said to Shaphan: **Have Hilkiah read this verse.** "I have found the Book of the Law in the temple of the LORD" (2 Kings 22:8). After all these years, the priest had found a copy of God's Word. It was like finding hidden treasure. Hilkiah gave the copy to Shaphan to take to King Josiah.

When Shaphan got back to the palace, he informed the king about the book. The king asked Shaphan to read the book aloud to him. Just like how Shaphan read God's Word, let's have someone read aloud what the Bible says happened next. **Have the narrator read this verse:** "When the king heard the words of the Book of the Law, he tore his robes" (2 Kings 22:11). **Continue with the story.** That meant that the words the king heard made him feel sorry for all the wicked deeds he had done and for not following God's laws. Then he ordered the priests to ask God what the people should do because they had not been obeying God's Word for so many years. Josiah was very sorrowful to learn that the people had sinned against God and he was afraid that God would punish them for their wickedness.

Hilkiah the priest went to talk to a prophetess named Huldah who had been faithful to God for many years. Huldah said to him, "The LORD is going to punish the people because of their disobedience. But because you and the king humbled yourselves before God when you heard His words, you and the people who are alive today will not see any disaster. God will give you peace."

What was the king's response when Hilkiah told him these words from the prophetess? He gathered all the leaders of the nation in the temple and read aloud the words from the Book of the Law. He told everyone there that he planned on following God's laws with all his heart.

Then this is what the leaders did. **Have the narrator read the verse:** "Then all the people pledged themselves to the covenant" (2 Kings 23:3). **Continue with the story.** (A covenant is an agreement between God and His people which was written in the Bible.) The king, priests, and the leaders tore down all the idols. There were thousands and thousands of idols and places where people had worshiped false gods. The king also got rid of all the priests who led the worship of the idols.

When all this was done, the king gave an order to all the people. **Have the king read the verse:** "Celebrate the Passover to the LORD your God, as it is written in this Book of the Covenant" (2 Kings 23:21).

Continue with the story. This is what the Bible says about the celebration that took place: **Have the narrator read this verse.** "Not since the days of the judges who led Israel, nor throughout the days of the kings of Israel and the kings of Judah, had any such Passover been observed. But in the eighteenth year of King Josiah, this Passover was celebrated to the LORD in Jerusalem" (2 Kings 23:22,23). **Continue with the story.** This was the greatest celebration for God since the Passover had been given in Egypt in the time of Moses!

This is what the Bible says about King Josiah: **Have the narrator read this verse.** "Neither before nor after Josiah was there a king like him who turned to the LORD as he did—with all his heart and with all his soul and with all his strength, in accordance with all the Law of Moses" (2 Kings 23:25).

Continue with the story. What a glorious tribute to a king who served God with all his heart! And it all started because one priest found a copy of God's Word in the temple and the king read it before the people. That is the power of God's Word! It changes lives; it changes history. It brings God's blessing to people who obey it!

- What had happened to the people when they lost the Book of the Law? (*They became wicked and their kings worshiped idols.*)

- Why do you think God was so pleased with King Josiah? (*Because he obeyed God. Because he followed God's Word.*)

- What happened when the people turned back to the Word of God? (*They celebrated. God was pleased with them. They were happy. They threw away all the idols.*)

- Josiah was only eight years old when he became king. What does that say about the importance of serving God when you're young? (*Josiah already had it in his heart that he wanted to serve God so he could grow up to be a good king. God could teach him things all his life because he started out loving God so early.*)

- What does serving God when you're young mean to you right now? (*I'm not too young to serve God right now. I need to follow God even though I'm not grown up.*)

- What does this story tell you about the importance of God's Word in the life of a person your age? (*I need God's Word just as much as an adult does. God's Word has power in my life too. God wants me to read His Word.*)

Did you notice that the king read God's Word aloud to his people? We don't do that too often in our culture. We do hear the Word of God read aloud when our pastor gives a sermon or when we are in Sunday school class or in another group at church. But we should also read it aloud in our homes and with our friends.

That's why I selected some of you to read the verses aloud when we came to them. Let's practice reading God's Word aloud some more. I'm sure we'll hear the power in God's Word when we do. These verses tell us something important about the power in God's Word.

Select good readers to read the following verses aloud in their strongest voices. Have students pick out the phrases used for God's Word after each passage.

Ephesians 6:17 (*Sword of the Spirit*)

Philippians 2:14–16 (*Word of Life*)

Hebrews 5:12–14 (*God's word*)

Truly, the Bible is a gift from God. We must treat it like our treasured possession.

LESSON ACTIVITY: The Bible Changes Our Lives

 Before Class: Write each of the five sets of verse references on a separate sheet of paper.

The Bible is not only a precious treasure, but it has great power too. Just as in the story we heard about King Josiah, the Bible changes lives. It has changed lives since the time it was written.

We are going to look at two aspects of the Bible's power: 1) What does it do in our lives? 2) How do we understand it?

Divide students into five groups. Give each group a Bible, a sheet with a pair of verses, and a pencil. (The answers in italic are for your reference.)

1. **1 John 2:5** (*When we obey God's Word, His love is in us.*)

   John 12:48 (*We will be judged by what is written in God's Word.*)

2. **Romans 10:17** (*Our faith comes from hearing God's Word.*)

   John 15:3 (*God's Word makes us clean.*)

3. **1 Peter 1:23** (*We are born again—become a part of God's family—through God's Word.*)

   John 8:31,32 (*We learn the truth and become free through God's Word.*)

4. **John 17:17** (*We are sanctified—set apart for God—by His Word.*)

   1 Peter 2:2 (**"milk" refers to God's Word**) (*We grow spiritually by studying God's Word.*)

5. **Hebrews 4:12** (*The Word of God judges our thoughts and attitudes.*)

   Revelation 1:3 (*We are blessed by God when we hear and do God's Word.*)

What does the Bible do in our lives? It does many things. Look up the Bible references your group has been given. In each reference, identify one thing that God's Word does in our lives, and write it down. Be prepared to tell the class what you have found.

Give groups time to read and write. Circulate and help groups that are having difficulty coming up with ideas. Then gather as a class and have each group read their verses and report what they found. As each verse is reported, list the students' ideas on the board and summarize with the italicized answers above. (You might want to have each group write their ideas on the board as they report.)

No other book can claim to do all that the Bible does. It is a supernatural book. But even as you read your verses in your group, you may have had a hard time understanding what was in them.

- Why do you think it's hard to understand God's Word? (*God wrote it and He thinks a lot deeper than we do. We don't know everything God does.*)

God tells us that humans, even the smartest ones, cannot understand all that He knows. God's knowledge is far above ours. **Read 1 Corinthians 2:7–12.**

- What does God tell us to do to help us understand His Word? (*We have to ask God's Spirit to reveal it to us. God's Spirit will help us understand what it means.*)

- Do you think a person who is not a Christian and not a member of God's family can understand the Bible? Why? (*No, because that person doesn't have the Holy Spirit helping him understand the Bible.*)

No one on earth can understand God's Word by himself. God's Spirit must help us. **Read 1 Corinthians 2:14.** This is why we must be careful to study the Bible and to ask God to help us understand it.

But we can learn some ways to help our Bible study become better. In our Application, we will learn one of these ways.

APPLICATION: A Topical Study on Truth
Divide students into groups of three or four. Distribute a "To Tell the Truth" handout and pencil to each student.

There are many ways to study the Bible. Let me explain a couple. In a *biographical study*, you would study the life of a person like Moses, David, or even Jesus. To do a *book study*, you would study a whole book of the Bible like Genesis. In a *chapter study*, you would study one chapter of the Bible like Psalm 23. A book study and a chapter study are similar except for how much of the Bible is being studied at one time. Today, we are going to try another specific way to study the Bible. It is called a *topical study*.

Many of you have written research papers or reports. Before you start, you need to pick out a topic. Your topic may have been an important person, animal habitats, or papermaking. There are many research topics for you to choose from. The same thing can be applied to a topical study of the Bible. You must choose a topic to begin your study.

Look at your handout. A few suggestions are listed at the top of the page under "Topic." Who will read them for me? **Choose a volunteer to read them.** This is only a small sample to get you started. I have chosen the topic "truth" to begin our study. Write "truth" in the blank beside the word "Topic." Now look at the list of tools. In a topical study, you can use these tools to discover what the Bible says about that topic. Check off the tools that you know you will have available to you at home.

If you have brought a topical Bible, Bible dictionary, and concordance to class, show your students how to use them. If you don't have these resources available, explain a concordance by using one in the back of a Bible. Also, explain that a Bible dictionary is like a regular dictionary except that all its words are about or found in the Bible. Many children's Bibles have a concordance and dictionary combined. Explain how to use each tool. Hand out one Bible with a concordance to each group. Have groups look up the word "truth" in the concordance.

 Teaching Tip: Make sure the Bible concordances you select contain the entry "truth."

Now you are ready to start your topical study. On your chart in the section labeled "Today's Lesson," you'll see two verses in that column. Look in your concordance under "truth," and fill in the blank with another verse on truth. Then look up all three verses and answer the questions. **Give groups time to do this, then discuss the questions together in class. Answers to the questions about the two verses listed are: (1) God's Word or the Bible; (2) Eternal; (3) It sets you free.**

Doing this activity helps us understand better what a topical Bible study is all about.

CHECK FOR UNDERSTANDING: Initial It
Divide students into pairs. Give each pair a dry-erase marker or piece of chalk. Write these categories across the board, spacing them as far apart as possible: Topical, Book, Chapter, Biographical.

We learned several different ways to do a Bible study. I have written those ways on the board. **Briefly review each kind of Bible study.**

I will name a subject for a type of Bible study. You and your partner will go up to the board and write your initials under the type of Bible study you think it is.

Name each of the following Bible study subjects. Give pairs time to identify each one. The type is in parentheses for your information. Note the types below that fit into two categories. After you have given students time to mark their answers, explain how both answers could be correct.

Genesis *(Book Study)*
The apostle Paul *(Biographical Study)*
Psalm 23 *(Chapter Study)*
The prophet Elijah *(Biographical Study)*
Wisdom *(Topical Study)*
Revelation 22 *(Chapter Study)*
Revelation *(Book or Topical Study)*
Creation *(Topical Study)*
Ruth *(Book or Biographical Study)*
Ruth 4 *(Chapter Study)*
Satan *(Biographical Study)*
Heaven *(Topical Study)*

You did well. I think you're getting the idea of the different ways to study the Bible. **Acknowledge pairs who did well in this exercise.**

MEMORY VERSE ACTIVITY: It's in the Bag

Hebrews 4:12—"For the Word of God is living and active. Sharper than any double-edged sword, it penetrates even to dividing soul and spirit, joints and marrow; it judges the thoughts and attitudes of the heart."

Before Class: You will be placing individual words on "gold coin" circles. If your group is very mature, write one word from the verse per coin (you will need 35 circles for each set). Otherwise, you can combine several words on each coin. (Include capital letters and punctuation so that it will be easier for the students to assemble the coins.) Cut enough circles out of the yellow construction paper to make two sets of coins.

Put each set of word coins in a bag. Divide the students into two teams and give each team a bag.

We have learned today that the Bible is God's Word and is very powerful. This makes every word very valuable, our treasure. Our memory verse today talks about how powerful God's Word is. In these bags are paper coins with today's verse on them. The goal is for your team to put the treasure coins in order so they spell out the verse correctly. We will see which team can put the verse together with the least amount of errors.

Give teams a couple of minutes to assemble their coins. Let them know when the time is about to expire. Then have each team read its verse aloud. While you read the verse from the Bible, have teams count the errors they made and then put their verse in the correct order. Have students read it together correctly a couple of times while including the reference.

This verse tells us that God's Word is so powerful that it can penetrate and change your thoughts and attitudes. Now that you know the correct order of the verse, put the coins back in the sack. Choose three people from your team to put the coins in the correct order. They will be competing against three members from the other team. When I say "go," both teams will put the coins in order. When your team members finish, your whole team will say the reference, Hebrews 4:12, together. I will make sure the verse is correct. If it isn't, I will ask your team to try again. The first team to finish correctly receives a point. The winning team will read the verse together as the other team follows along and puts the coins in the correct order.

Follow this process. Allow other team members to take turns. When everyone has had a turn, ask individuals to recite the verse to you.

WEEKLY ASSIGNMENT: What's the Truth?

In their Bible Reading Journals, have students write the heading "Books of Poetry" followed by the book names: Job, Psalms, Proverbs, Ecclesiastes, Song of Solomon. They will be memorizing the names of these five books this week.

Have students record the following daily reading assignments in their journals:

Day 1—Job 2
Day 2—Job 3
Day 3—Psalm 1
Day 4—Psalm 23
Day 5—Proverbs 4
Day 6—Proverbs 10
Day 7—Ecclesiastes 12

This week, you will continue your topical study about truth using your handout. Each day you will look up verses about truth. Notice that days 1 to 4 have two verses listed. There is a blank for you to add another verse, just as you did today. There are also questions for you to answer each day. On days 5 and 6, you will notice that this spot is blank. On those days, use a concordance to find your own verses on truth to look up and write those verses here. Bring your handout with you next week to share what you learned.

 Teaching Tip: Make copies of the page containing "truth" from a good concordance to give to students who do not have a concordance available.

To Tell the Truth

Bible Study—Topical

Topic: _____

(grace, **truth**, prayer, faith assurance, justification, peace)

Check off the tools you have:

☐ Bible   ☐ Topical Bible   ☐ Bible Dictionary

☐ Concordance   ☐ Notebook   ☐ _____

Look in your Bible concordance and find verses listed for the topic you have chosen:

	Verses	Questions
Today's Lesson	Psalm 119:160 John 8:31,32 _____	What is **truth** in these passages? What is said about **truth**? What does **truth** do for you?
Day 1	John 14:6 John 1:14,17 _____	What is **truth** in these passages? What is said about **truth**? What does **truth** do for you?
Day 2	John 16:13 John 14:17 _____	What is **truth** in these passages? What is said about **truth**? What does **truth** do for you?

	Verses	Questions
Day 3	1 John 3:18 Ephesians 4:15 _____	What should we do **truthfully**? Give some examples of this.
Day 4	2 John 4 3 John 4, 8 _____	What do you think it means "to walk in the **truth**"? What does this bring to others?
Day 5	Look up your own verses on the topic. _____ _____ _____	Write what these verses say.
Day 6	Look up your own verses on the topic. _____ _____ _____	Write what these verses say.

Book of Wisdom

LESSON PLAN

OBJECTIVE: Students will begin establishing good habits of regular, systematic study of the Bible.

APPLICATION: Students will use biographical and chapter Bible study methods.

LESSON PLAN ELEMENT	ACTIVITY	TIME	SUPPLIES
Opening Activity	*A Revealing Light*	6–8	Lemon juice; Q-tip swabs; 2 lamps without shades; white paper; paper cups
Memory Verse Activity	*Search Lights*	3–5	2 flashlights; 2 crosses; 2 Bibles; 2 lamps from Opening Activity; 2 shoes; 2 candles; 2 cups of dirt; dry-erase marker or chalk
Bible Story—Psalm 119, Chapter Bible study	*Apples of Wisdom*	10–15	Bibles; 2 different Bible translations; "Shaking the Tree" handouts, part 1; 3 copies of "Apples of Wisdom"; tape; markers; scissors
Lesson Activity	*The Bible Hold*	6–8	Bibles
Check for Understanding	*Five Finger Facts for a Firm Grip*	3–5	Bibles
Application	*Jonah's Journey*	10–15	Bibles; pencils; "Shaking the Tree" handouts, part 2
Weekly Assignment	*Shaking the Tree Again*	2–4	"Shaking the Tree" handouts, part 1

Before I (Bill Bright) became a believer in Jesus Christ, God's Word didn't make any sense to me. I tried to read it occasionally during my high school years and college days, but found it boring. Finally, I concluded that no really intelligent person could believe the Bible.

But when I became a Christian, my life was transformed, and my attitudes concerning the Scriptures changed. I realized that the Bible was truly the holy, inspired Word of God. For over fifty years it has been more important to me than the thousands of books in my library combined.

Why is the Bible so important to the Christian? There are five basic reasons.

First, *the Word of God is divinely inspired.* Paul writes, "All Scripture is God-breathed and is useful for teaching, rebuking, correcting and training in righteousness, so that the man of God may be thoroughly equipped for every good work" (2 Timothy 3:16).

Second, *the Scripture is the basis of our belief.* As the divinely inspired Word, the Bible gives us God's perspective on how we should live. It offers His pardon for our sins, reveals His purpose for our lives, shows us how to live peacefully in a world of turmoil, and commands us to be filled with His Spirit so we can be fruitful witnesses for our Lord Jesus Christ.

Many years ago, while I was a student at Fuller Theological Seminary, two gifted young evangelists came to speak during our chapel program. Both believed and preached the Word of God without questioning its authority. Later, however, they began to doubt that the Bible was truly inspired in every word.

One of these men finally rejected the integrity of the Scripture altogether. As a result, he had no moorings on which to base his life and ministry. He is now a skeptic and an outspoken opponent of the Christian faith.

The other young evangelist chose to believe that the Bible is truly the authoritative, inspired Word of God, and what he could not understand he entrusted to God and believed by faith.

Few remember the name of the first man. But the second is Billy Graham, whom God has used to touch the lives of millions around the world.

Third, *the Bible is God's love letter to man.* From Genesis to Revelation, it tells of God's great compassion for us and of His desire to have fellowship with us. John 3:16 summarizes the depth of His love for us: "God so loved the world that he gave his one and only Son, that whoever believes in him shall not perish but have eternal life."

Fourth, *the Bible reveals God's attributes.* It tells us that He is holy, sovereign, righteous, and just; that He is loving, merciful, and kind; that He is gracious, patient, and faithful.

Fifth, *God's Word teaches us how to live holy lives and to be fruitful witnesses for our Lord.* The more we read and meditate on His precious Word—and let His Holy Spirit control our lives—the more fruitful we become.

Studying the Bible is a lifelong adventure. For your students, it will be the most life-changing habit they can develop. Ask God to help them learn how to dig into His Word on their own so that they will not be totally dependent on others for their spiritual growth. At the same time, I encourage you to depend on God's Word for your daily Christian living and as a model to your students.

LESSON PLAN

OPENING ACTIVITY: A Revealing Light

Before Class: Using lemon juice and Q-tip swabs, write each word of the phrase "Bible is a Light" on a separate sheet of paper. Number the sheets from 1 to 4 to keep the message in order. Set up three or four work areas with paper, swabs, and cups of lemon juice. Put the lamps on a front table, and make sure they are plugged in.

Review the names of the Poetry Books. Then talk to your students about their Bible Reading Journal, asking them what they learned since the last session.

Go over what the students learned through their topical study on truth.

Begin the lesson by saying: Light is very important to us.

- Can you think of ways that light helps us? (*It makes plants grow. We can see things with light. It affects our moods. It guides us. It makes things warm.*)

Another thing that light does is to reveal things that we can't normally see. When searching for something we've lost, we shine a light on it. When a jeweler wants to see small writing on jewelry, he shines a light on it.

Hold up the four pieces of paper with the invisible words written in lemon juice. I have here what appear to be four blank sheets of paper. But let's see what our light reveals. **Give sheet #1 to a student. Have him or her hold it close to the light bulb until the word** *Bible* **is revealed. Do this with the other three sheets.**

Our lamp revealed the message that the "Bible is a light." **Read Psalm 119:105.** This verse tells us that the Bible acts as our guide as we go through life. Just as a light helps us walk down a dark path without stumbling, the Bible shows us what to avoid as we go through our day. It reveals many things we need to change and shows us the things we are doing well. Just as we wouldn't walk down a dark, unknown path without a light, we need to use our Bibles every day as we walk the path of life.

Divide students into three or four groups and instruct them to go to the work areas. Have each student take a piece of paper and a Q-tip swab. Using a Q-tip for your pen and lemon juice for the ink, write a word or two telling how God's Word helps us. It might be to tell us to be kind to a brother or sister, to obey our parents, or to listen to those in authority at school like teachers and administrators. When it dries, give your slip to someone else in your group, and let that person put it in front of the lamp to reveal what you wrote.

Give students a few minutes to do this.

Teaching Tip: Make sure that students do not touch the bare light bulb with their hands. Also, monitor the activity to ensure students don't leave paper near the hot bulb too long or it will burn.

MEMORY VERSE ACTIVITY: Search Lights

Psalm 119:105—"Your word is a lamp to my feet and a light for my path."

Before Class: Hide two flashlights, two crosses, two Bibles, two lamps, two shoes, two candles, and two cups of dirt in separate places around the room.

Write the verse on the board or posterboard. Divide the class into two groups.

Read the verse together as a class. Our verse today compares the Bible to a light. It is saying that the Word of God guides us and helps us find our way through life just as a flashlight searches a room for hidden items.

Darken the lights in the room. To help us learn this verse, we will play a "Search Lights" game. I have hidden objects around the room that represent one or more words in the verse. **Give a flashlight to each team.** We will use our Search Lights to find the items that will help us remember the memory verse. The first item to find is a cross. It represents God.

Give the two students time to each find a cross. When they return, say: This cross represents the first word in our verse, "Your." Let's say the word together: "Your."

Give the flashlight to another member from each team. Have them search for the Bibles. When they return, say: This Bible represents the word "word" in our verse. Let's all say it together: "word."

Hold up the cross and the Bible as your students say, "Your Word."

Give the flashlight to another member from each team. Have them search for the lamps. When they return, say: This lamp represents the phrase "is a lamp." Let's say it all together: "is a lamp."

Hold up a cross, a Bible, and a lamp as your students say, "Your Word is a lamp."

Give the flashlight to another member from each team. Have them search for the shoes. When they return, say: This shoe represents the phrase "to my feet." Let's all say it together: "to my feet."

Hold up a cross, a Bible, a lamp, and a shoe as your students say, "Your Word is a lamp to my feet."

Give the flashlight to another member from each team. Have them search for the candles. When they return, say: This candle represents the phrase "and a light." Let's all say it together: "and a light."

Hold up a cross, a Bible, a lamp, a shoe, and a candle as the students say, "Your Word is a lamp to my feet and a light."

Give the flashlight to another member from each team. Have them search for the cups of dirt. When they return, say: The cup of dirt represents the phrase "for my path." Let's all say it together: "for my path."

Hold up a cross, a Bible, a lamp, a shoe, a candle, and a cup of dirt. Have students say, "Your Word is a lamp to my feet and a light for my path."

Go through all the items one more time, and have the students add the reference at the end when they repeat the verse.

If you choose to do so, hide the items again. Select twelve students to do the search and have them step out of the room while the other students hide the items. When the search is over, you can have individual students recite the verse to you.

When finished, say: In our Bible story today, we are going to learn more reasons why the Bible is so important to us and why we really need it!

BIBLE STORY: Apples of Wisdom

Teaching Tip: This may be a good time to purchase Bibles for students who do not have them. Select a Bible that has a good concordance in the back and a translation that is easy for your students to read. Present the Bible with great honor so the students know how wonderful it is to receive a Bible.

Before Class: Draw a tree with branches on the board. Make enough branches so that your students can tape a dozen apples on it from the "Apples of Wisdom" handouts. If possible, copy the "Apples of Wisdom" reproducible onto light red paper, and copy the two parts of "Shaking the Tree" on the front and back of another piece of paper. Cut out the apples.

During our previous class, we learned how to do a topical Bible study. You did very well in your study about truth. When you examined the Bible for information about truth, the Bible "lit" up your mind with new facts about God's truth. That's how the Bible serves as a light for you. Whenever you desire, you can use the other topics on your "To Tell the Truth" page to do another topical Bible study.

There are many ways we can describe how wonderful the Bible is to us. Martin Luther, a famous Christian who lived many years ago, described Bible study like picking apples. He said:

Search the Bible as a whole, shaking the whole tree. Read it rapidly, as you would any other book. Then shake every limb—study book after book.

Then shake every branch, giving attention to the chapters when they do not break the sense. Then shake each twig by a careful study of the paragraphs and sentences. And you will be rewarded if you will look under each leaf by searching the meaning of the words.

Do you see how studying the Bible is like shaking an apple tree? Each time you study, you pick more "apples" of truth. Every time you and I study God's Word carefully, we are building up our storehouse of faith. When we memorize the Word, our faith is being increased. That's why we are learning different methods of Bible study.

For our Bible story today, we're going to do something different. I want to teach you how to do a chapter Bible study. We will not be doing a book study because it is similar to a chapter study but just takes a lot longer. You can wait until you're a little older to do a complete book study.

Teaching Tip: Introduce two translations that are commonly used in your church. This curriculum uses the *New International Version,* so that should be one of the versions you select. Also, check to see what translations your students bring with them to class. Some children bring Bible-story books that look like Bibles. Explain the difference between a Bible-story book and a complete Bible. A Bible-story book retells stories of the Bible but does not use the Bible's exact words. A complete Bible gives all the chapters and verses of the Bible.

In our last lesson, we learned about different tools we could use for our Bible study. They are a Bible dictionary, a Bible concordance, and a topical Bible. Now we will learn about different Bible translations. **Hold up two different translations.** Since the Bible writers did not write in English, the Bible has to be translated so we can understand it. There are many translations of the Bible. Some are better than others. Let me show you two translations. **Show your translations.**

To do our chapter study, we are going to look at Psalm 119. We're going to be "shaking the tree" like Martin Luther said. We will be finding "apples of wisdom."

The Psalms are part of the five Books of Poetry. The five Books of Poetry in the Old Testament are: Job, Psalms, Proverbs, Ecclesiastes, and Song of Solomon. The Psalms are some of the most often quoted poetry in the world. The book of Psalms is in the middle of your Bible. Turn to Psalm 119.

Distribute the "Shaking the Tree" handouts and markers. On your handout, you will see several questions. These are the questions to ask when doing a chapter study. That doesn't mean that each question will be answered in the chapter, but most of them will be.

Before we start, let's pray and ask the Holy Spirit to sharpen our minds to understand what God says to us in this Bible study. **Pray, asking the Holy Spirit to illuminate the Scriptures for each person in the class.**

Distribute the twelve "Apples" among the students. (Depending on how many students you have, some students may not get an apple and some may get more than one.)

Read Psalm 119:1–16 aloud. Then read each of the questions one at a time. Help the students answer each question. Have one student with an apple write the answer on the apple using a marker, and then tape the apple to the tree. When you finish the activity, you will have twelve apples taped to the tree.

Optional Activity: Make a tree by twisting ropes of brown butcher paper and assembling the ropes to form a trunk and branches. Place the tree in your classroom. Tape the apples to the tree during the Bible Story. During other class sessions, repeat the chapter Bible study activity with other chapters and replace the apples to make a new "crop of wisdom."

The following are suggested answers for the questions on the handout:

- What is the main subject of the chapter? *(God's Word.)*

- What is the main lesson? *(We must follow the rules in God's Word.)*

- What is the key verse? *(Psalm 119:11.)*

- Who are the main characters? *(The person writing the Psalm; God; people who keep God's Word.)*

- What does the chapter teach about God the Father? *(God has given us laws that He expects us to obey.)*

- What does the chapter teach about Jesus Christ? *(Not specifically mentioned.)*

- What does the chapter teach about the Holy Spirit? *(Not specifically mentioned.)*

- Is there any example to follow? *(Follow the example of the writer of the psalm who obeys God's laws and hides God's Word in his heart.)*

- Is there any error for me to avoid? *(Do not stray from God's Word. Do not neglect it.)*

- Is there any duty for me to do? *(Keep God's Word so my way is pure.)*

- Is there any promise for me to claim? *(God will bless me if I keep His Word.)*

- Is there any prayer for me to pray? *(I could pray verses 12–16 as praise to God.)*

When you finish placing the apples on the tree, discuss the following questions:

- Although we did only a portion of a chapter today, what do you think was hard about doing a chapter Bible study like this? *(I have to read a lot of verses. I'm not sure I can answer all the questions correctly.)*

- What did you like about this Bible study method? *(I like having questions to answer so I can think about the chapter better. I like sticking to one part of the Bible instead of looking at verses in several places.)*

- How would you summarize what the writer of Psalm 119 thinks about God's Word? *(He loves and wants to obey it. He says everyone who obeys it will be blessed.)*

For your weekly assignment, you will be studying more of Psalm 119. But right now, let's see why it's so important to use different ways of getting to know the Bible well.

LESSON ACTIVITY: The Bible Hold

 Teaching Tip: Complete Bibles rather than New Testaments work best for this activity.

As you probably already know, the Bible is essential for a believer to live a strong spiritual life.

- Why do you think the Bible is so important to our everyday life? *(We get to know God better when we read the Bible. The Bible helps us know how to live.)*

- How has using your Bible Reading Journal helped you? *(It helps me remember to pray and obey God's commands. I am reading about things in the Bible I never knew before.)*

We need to use our Bibles every day. There are five different ways we can learn the Word of God. We are going to learn these methods through an activity called "The Bible Hold."

Make sure each student has a Bible. Hold up your Bible in your hand with a firm grip. **Give students a moment to do this.** Notice that it takes all five fingers to get a strong grip on the book. Now set your Bible aside so we can do a finger-fact count.

Hold up your fingers. **Point to the appropriate finger as you refer to it**. The little finger represents *hearing* the Word of God. Your ring finger represents *reading* the Word of God. The middle finger represents *studying* the Bible. The index finger represents *memorizing* Bible verses, and the thumb represents *meditating* on what the Bible says. Let's say these facts in order as we point to each appropriate finger: hearing, reading, studying, memorizing, and meditating.

Now, put your fingers down. Let's consider each of these activities. Think about hearing and meditating first.

- What is the difference between hearing and meditating on God's Word? *(Hearing is listening to the words and meditating is thinking about them deeply or for a long time.)*

Usually, we hear God's Word at church during a Sunday school lesson or a sermon. We may also hear the Word of God on the radio, television, or a tape. When we hear the Bible, we may think about it or meditate on it right away or even later during the week. Meditating is thinking about something deeply or for a long time.

Hearing God's Word is important to our Christian life. Romans 10:17 says that "faith comes from hearing" the Word of God. That's why it's so important to go to church regularly. We build our faith through hearing.

But just hearing and meditating do not give us a good strong grip on the Word of God. Try picking up your Bible with your thumb and little finger. **Give students time to try a two-finger grip.** Now grab your Bible with the same two fingers on your other hand. **Give**

students time to do this. Wasn't that difficult? We must do more than hear and meditate. We cannot expect to know God's Word well if we only hear it at church and don't do anything more.

Another way to learn God's Word is by reading it for ourselves. This helps us tremendously and is essential to our spiritual growth. We have been doing this through our Bible Reading Journal.

- Why do you think it's so important to read the Word of God for ourselves? *(When we read something for ourselves, we remember it better. We can read the Bible anytime, even if we aren't at church.)*

Statistics tell us that we remember about 25 percent of what we read. Now, pick up your Bible with your thumb, little finger, and ring finger. When we add personal reading to hearing and meditating, we get a firmer grip on God's Word, but our hold is still weak. Again, try grabbing the Bible with your other hand using the same three fingers. It is probably a little difficult, but you can do it. **Give students time to try this hold.**

The fourth way we can learn God's Word is by studying it.

- Why do you think it's important to study the Word of God even if you are hearing, meditating on, and reading the Bible? *(Studying means looking at it more closely. Studying helps me remember things better.)*

Did you know that you remember up to 50 percent of what you study? That's why teachers give tests in school. They know that when you study the material, you will remember and understand it much better—even years later. When you get ready to take a test over a chapter in a book, you study it really hard. You may have already read it once, but you know that to really remember what the material is all about, you must take more time with it.

It's the same with God's Word. When you study God's Word, you may underline important facts, write outlines, and do word studies. You might make notes in the Bible's margin or look at chapter and paragraph outlines prepared by Bible scholars. You may make a list of many details in the portion of the Bible that you are studying. In our last lesson, we learned how to do a word study by using a concordance. There are many good ways to study the Bible.

The last way to learn more about God's Word is by memorizing verses.

- Why do you think it's so important to memorize God's Word? *(You can take part of God's Word with you wherever you are. So you can use what you learn better.)*

Just like a good football or basketball player memorizes his plays, so we must memorize important verses in God's Word. We should memorize verses that are essential—ones that we don't want to forget or that give us information on how to live our lives.

Now hold up your Bible, but this time use all five fingers. **Give students a moment to do this.** Can you feel how much firmer your grip is? In a similar way, "The Bible Hold" is a strong way to learn God's Word.

CHECK FOR UNDERSTANDING: Five Finger Facts for a Firm Grip

In our Lesson Activity, we learned five ways to know God's Word. This five-finger hold gives us a good grip on the Bible. Starting with the little finger, let's say these five facts. **Have students repeat after you: hearing, reading, studying, memorizing, meditating.** Now turn to your neighbor and recite the five-finger facts. **Give students time to do this.**

Now let's number our fingers from 1 to 5 starting with our little finger. When I say a number, see if you can tell me which finger fact it represents. **Call out various numbers.**

Remember, as you spend time in God's Word this week, you should be using all five of these methods to get a firm grip on God's Word.

APPLICATION: Jonah's Journey

This week, we are memorizing the Major Prophets in the Old Testament. Next week, we will begin memorizing the Minor Prophets. Remember, the reason that the Minor Prophets are called "minor" is not because they are less important but because the Minor Prophet books are shorter.

One wonderful way to study the Bible is to study a person in the Bible. There are 2,930 people mentioned in the Bible. The lives of many of these people make extremely interesting biographical studies. "Biographical" refers to a person's life. The biography of the person we are going to study today is in a Minor Prophet book. His name is Jonah.

First, read aloud the Book of Jonah. Then go through Part 2 of the "Shaking the Tree" handout. If you think your students are mature enough to do the questions on their own, pair them and have them work together. Otherwise, go through the questions as a group. Possible answers are given below. Accept any good answers from your students.

- What was the place and situation in which he lived? *(A long distance from Nineveh, probably in Israel.)*

- How did that affect his life? *(He didn't like the people of Nineveh because he was an Israelite.)*

- What do we know about this person's family? *(He was the son of Amittai.)*

- What kind of training did he have? *(He was God's prophet so he must have had religious training.)*

- What great things did this person do during his or her life? *(He told the sailors about God and they believed in God. He preached to the people of Nineveh, and they repented.)*

- Was there a big crisis? If so, how did he face it? *(When God told Jonah to go to Nineveh, he didn't want to go so he ran away by sailing on a ship.)*

- What were this person's outstanding character traits? *(Disobedient at times—he disobeyed God when God told him to go to Nineveh. He was brave—he told the sailors to throw him overboard because he knew it was his fault that the storm was wrecking the ship. He listened—after the big fish vomited him up on the beach, he finally went to Nineveh. He complained—when the people of Nineveh repented, he complained about it to God.)*

- Who were his friends? What kind of people were they? *(Sailors on the ship to Tarshish. They didn't believe in God.)*

- What influence did these friends have on him? *(They woke Jonah up and told him the ship was going to sink because of the storm. They wanted him to call on his God to save them.)*

- What influence did he have on these friends? *(Jonah admitted that the storm was his fault and that his God was the true God. When they threw Jonah overboard after he had told them to do that, they believed in God because the storm went away immediately.)*

- Does this person's life show any change for the good or for the bad? *(He did finally listen to God and go to Nineveh, but he wasn't that happy about obeying God.)*

- What was his experience with God? Notice prayer life, faith, service to God, knowledge of God's Word, courage in telling others about God, and attitude toward the worship of God. *(Jonah prayed in the belly of the fish. He also prayed because he was angry when God didn't destroy the people of Nineveh. He didn't have much faith because he was too worried about his own welfare. He served God by preaching to the people of Nineveh. He knew God had told him to go to Nineveh. He told the sailors about the true God. He prayed a prayer that showed he knew God was able to save him from the belly of the fish. He preached to the people in Nineveh about how God would punish the wicked.)*

- Was there any outstanding sin or faults in this person's life? How was this sin committed? How did this sin affect his life? *(He felt sorry for himself. He didn't have compassion on the people of Nineveh. He didn't do what God told him to do until God made his life very difficult.)*

- What were his children like? *(Doesn't say.)*

- What lessons can you learn from studying this person's life? *(Obey God right away. Preach about Jesus so that people can become part of God's family and avoid punishment. Don't feel sorry for myself. Remember that God is in charge of my life and He can see me wherever I go.)*

WEEKLY ASSIGNMENT: Shaking the Tree Again

This week students will memorize the names of the Major Prophets: Isaiah, Jeremiah, Lamentations, Ezekiel, Daniel.

Have students record these daily reading assignments in their journals:

Day 1—Isaiah 1
Day 2—Isaiah 6
Day 3—Jeremiah 1
Day 4—Lamentations 5
Day 5—Ezekiel 1 and 2
Day 6—Daniel 1
Day 7—Daniel 6

You have now learned how to do three different types of Bible studies. Last week, we did a topical study of the word *truth*. In our Application, we did a biographical study of Jonah. In our Bible Story, we learned how to do a chapter study using the first verses of Psalm 119.

For our Weekly Assignment, I want you to continue your chapter study of Psalm 119 by looking at verses 17 through 32. You will be using the same questions you used for the first sixteen verses. **Pass out another copy of the "Shaking the Tree" handout, Part 1, or have students use their current sheet and add their new information for Psalm 119:17–32 beside the information for verses 1–16.**

Shaking the Tree – Part 1

Chapter Bible Study

Chapter you are studying:

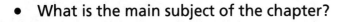

- What is the main subject of the chapter?

- What is the main lesson?

- What is the key verse?

- Who are the main characters?

- What does the chapter teach about God the Father?

- What does the chapter teach about Jesus Christ?

- What does the chapter teach about the Holy Spirit?

- Is there any example to follow?

- Is there any error for me to avoid?

- Is there any duty for me to do?

- Is there any promise for me to claim?

- Is there any prayer for me to pray?

Shaking the Tree – Part 2

Biographical Bible Study

Name of person you are studying:

_____

- What was the place and situation in which he or she lived?

- How did that affect his or her life?

- What do we know about this person's family?

- What kind of training did he or she have?

- What great things did this person do during his or her life?

- Was there a big crisis? If so, how did he or she face it?

- What were this person's outstanding character traits?

- Who were his or her friends? What kind of people were they?

- What influence did these friends have on him or her?

- What influence did he or she have on these friends?

- Does this person's life show any change for the good or for the bad?

- What was his or her experience with God? Notice prayer life, faith, service to God, knowledge of God's Word, courage in telling others about God, and attitude toward the worship of God.

- Was there any outstanding sin or faults in this person's life? How was this sin committed? How did this sin affect his or her life?

- What were his or her children like?

- What lessons can you learn from studying this person's life?

Apples of Wisdom

What's in the Old Testament?

BOOK OBJECTIVE	To provide a survey of the Bible.
UNIT OBJECTIVE	To introduce students to the Old Testament and how it points to Jesus Christ as the Messiah.
LESSON 5: The Drama Begins	*Objective:* To help students learn from biblical examples the importance of obedience in the Christian life. *Application:* To help students put into practice one way they can obey God in their daily lives.
LESSON 6: Law and Grace	*Objective:* To help students understand our inability to keep the law and our need for God's grace. *Application:* To encourage students to commit themselves to practicing the Law of Love in the classroom.
LESSON 7: Joshua and David	*Objective:* To help students learn to believe the promises of God and maintain fellowship with God, unhindered by sin. *Application:* To show students how to confess their sins and understand that their sin was forgiven.
LESSON 8: Elijah and Jeremiah	*Objective:* To show students how to serve God with power and courage. *Application:* To help students commit themselves to ways of being heroes for God.

Man has long searched for the Creator of life and the answers to his age-old questions: *Who am I? Why am I here? Where did I come from? Where am I going?*

In the story of man's creation recorded in the Book of Genesis, God gives us the answers. God created man with a free will—the ability to choose his own destiny—and put within him the principle and power of obedience. With the knowledge of God's will, the first man, Adam, knew the rewards of obedience and the penalty for disobedience. But would he obey?

As a test, God placed a tree in the Garden of Eden. Eating of its fruit would destroy Adam's innocence and enable him to know good and evil. But it would also result in his death and the Fall of the human race (Genesis 2:16,17).

I'm sure you know the familiar story—how the serpent, Satan, beguiled Eve, who then ate of the forbidden fruit and gave it to her husband. Knowing the consequences of his act, Adam chose to eat the fruit anyway. This act of disobedience caused "the Fall" of mankind from innocence and separated humanity from the loving Creator (Genesis 3). The after-effects were devastating. The Fall resulted in pain, hardship, and sorrow for man. Separated from God, man was condemned to eternal spiritual darkness. In the process, fear of God replaced fellowship with God, and shame over sin obscured the joy of innocence.

The Old Testament records the dramatic effects of the Fall—the rapid decline of humanity into a depravity so terrible that God regretted ever creating man. Therefore, God destroyed all but a small remnant of His creation in a global flood. Even with its fresh start in Noah and his family, humanity soon plunged the world into new depths of darkness.

The last book of the Old Testament, Malachi, presents God's final message to a disobedient people. Significantly, the last book of the Bible—the Book of Revelation—presents the final triumph of Christ the Messiah over evil and the ultimate restoration of man to his original destiny.

But God was not caught off guard by the sin of Adam. God had a wonderful plan. Not an afterthought of the Fall, it was a glorious work that He conceived before the creation of man (Ephesians 1:3–14). The plan involved God's unconditional love and perfect justice.

Man could not redeem himself. Only one who was without sin could satisfy the justice of God. The substitute had to be a Man to take the place of man. He had to be sinless to die for the sinner. Since humanity could not provide such a Redeemer, that Savior had to come from God.

To this purpose, God, in the person of His only Son, Jesus Christ, conceived by the Holy Spirit and born of a virgin, offered Himself as the required substitute.

The animal sacrifices of the Old Testament symbolized this. The Israelites brought their sacrifices—an unblemished lamb, dove, or bull—to the priest. The animal was slain, and its blood was sprinkled by the priest on the altar as a temporary covering for sin. This offering was a picture of the coming of God's one special Lamb (John 1:29), whose blood would not just temporarily cover man's sins, but would wash them away forever.

Both man's Fall and God's plan for restoration are found in the Old Testament. Woven inseparably into its tapestry, the redemption story demonstrates unmistakably the marvelous love and grace of God. In the pronouncement of judgment upon the serpent, in the faith and obedience of Abraham, in the leadership of Moses and the birth of the Hebrew nation, and in the voice of the prophets, we see clearly God's love call to humanity through His Son.

Throughout the Old Testament, the person and nature of God stands in contrast to the tragedy and consequences of sin. We see Him as the Creator, Sustainer, Judge, and Redeemer. And in this we can take heart: no matter how dark this world seems, God has a plan and He has included us in it if we will trust and obey Him.

The more we study the Old Testament, the better we will understand God's wonderful plan. I urge you to dig deeper into its events and truths, using the many resources available to you through your local Christian bookstore. And pass what you learn on to your students so that they too can be amazed at what God has done for them.

LESSON 5

The Drama Begins

LESSON PLAN

OBJECTIVE: Students will learn from biblical examples the importance of obedience in the Christian life.

APPLICATION: Students will put into practice one way they can obey God in their daily lives.

LESSON PLAN ELEMENT	ACTIVITY	TIME	SUPPLIES
Opening Activity	*Let's Create*	10–12	Glue; construction paper; toothpicks; various pasta; markers; small marshmallows; 3 or 4 boxes; 1 copy of "Creation" from "The Drama Begins" master
Bible Story—Genesis 3, Adam and Eve's fall	*The Big Fall*	10–15	White paper towels; cookie sheet or board; food coloring; eyedropper; 1 copy of "Adam and Eve" from "The Drama Begins" master
Lesson Activity	*Watch It Grow*	5–10	Shaving cream or Silly String can; cookie sheet; yardstick, ruler, or measuring tape; 1 copy of "Noah and the Ark" from "The Drama Begins" master
Application	*Obedience and Disobedience*	6–8	Bible; dry-erase marker or chalk; 1 copy of "Abraham and Isaac" from the "The Drama Begins" master
Check for Understanding	*Old Testament Time Line*	3–5	All pictures from "The Drama Begins"; butcher paper or newsprint; tape or sticky tack; scissors
Memory Verse Activity	*Verse Pairs*	3–5	Dry-erase marker or chalk
Weekly Assignment	*Order Please*	3–5	"Order Please" handouts; dry-erase marker or chalk

Genesis gives us a picture of man's origin, his Fall, and God's provision for his salvation. Man was created to have fellowship with God, but because of man's stubborn self-will, he chose to go his own independent way and fellowship with God was broken. This is what the Bible calls sin.

As a result of the Fall of Adam, all mankind inherited a sin nature. Paul writes, "Sin entered the world through one man, and death through sin, and in this way death came to all men, because all sinned" (Romans 5:12).

It is this first act in the drama of mankind that sets the stage for all that is to follow. If there had been no sin, there would have been no need for redemption, and no need for a Bible to tell us of the way of redemption.

The Fall of Adam not only affected man's relationship with God, but it caused a breach in human relationships. The downward course of human nature plunged even deeper with the murder of Abel by his brother, Cain.

As people began to forge a civilization without God, violence and death became constant realities in human existence. Man's wickedness became so vile that God regretted ever making a human being.

Finding only Noah and his family worthy of saving, God decided to destroy His creation by flood. Nevertheless, after the flood, man's inherent sin nature caused him to once again go his own willful way. This time, God met man's arrogance by confusing the language of evil people and scattering them over the face of the earth.

Even so, we see the redemptive heart of God at work in the story of Abraham and Isaac. The calling of Abraham brought the promise of salvation. Because Abraham obeyed God in faith and love, God was able to give him a promise of blessing to the world. The story of Abraham shows how God developed and tested Abraham's faith in relationship to the promise.

The chosen line went through Abraham and Isaac down to the promised Messiah, Jesus Christ, who fulfilled the promise of blessing and redemption. The lineage of Christ is part of the fabric of the Book of Genesis. Those selected to be in the line were chosen because they were people of faith like Abraham. Today, we who choose Jesus by faith have our part with faithful Abraham (Romans 4:16).

This lesson surveys the beginning of human history, including the creation of man, the Fall of Adam and Eve, Noah's ark, and Abraham's sacrifice of Isaac. To help your students begin to understand where each biblical event fits in the time sequence, your class will be making a time line. It will be used throughout this unit as more stories are added.

In all these lessons, references to or illustrations that foretell the life and death of Jesus will be emphasized to bring out the fact that Jesus is the central Person of the Bible.

LESSON PLAN

OPENING ACTIVITY: Let's Create!

 Before Class: Place the supply materials in boxes so they're ready to distribute. Set up three or four work areas around the room.

Cut apart the pictures from "The Drama Begins." Set aside the pictures of Adam and Eve, Noah, and Abraham and Isaac for later activities.

Divide students into three or four groups.

Most of us like to make things. It is very fun to be creative. We get a lot of satisfaction from making things ourselves.

- What are some things you have created? *(Lego creations; cooking recipes; bead bracelets; wooden birdhouses.)*

Today, you are going to get a chance to create a new creature or animal. I have set up some areas where you can work. **Assign students to the work areas. There should be nothing at these areas at this time. When students have all assembled at their areas, say:** Okay! Start creating!

Wait for dismay and questions about what materials they can use to create. Then say, We cannot create anything unless we have material to start with. But there was Someone who created everything out of nothing. **Read Genesis 1:1.** This verse tells us that in the beginning, before there was anything, God created heaven and earth. That means that He created them out of nothing. **Hold up the "Creation" picture from "The Drama Begins."** Only God can create out of nothing. We can't. We have to have something to start with.

Hand out the supply boxes to each group. Now you can create. Use these materials to make a new creature.

Give students 5 to 8 minutes to do this. Be sure to give them a warning before asking them to stop, so slow workers can adjust their plans. Then ask volunteers to show their creations.

For some of you, it was still hard to make a new creature even if you had materials to start with. You wanted to fashion your creature after animals you already know. But God made everything on our earth different. He didn't have a pattern to go by. Think of all the different animals there are in the world. How about all the different plants? God made each of them unique.

The last thing God created was man. **Read Genesis 1:31.** Some of you finished your creature and thought it looked good; others of you thought your creation wasn't that wonderful. When God finished creating the universe, He looked upon His work and saw it was good. But something would happen to change that goodness. Let's find out what that was in our Bible Story.

BIBLE STORY: The Big Fall

Before Class: Put several layers of paper towels on the cookie sheet or board. (The cookie sheet will protect your table from food coloring leaking onto it.) Mix several colors of food coloring drops (red, green, blue) until you get a dark, ugly color. Add a little water to the food coloring so that it will spread further when dropped onto the paper towels.

Have ready the "Adam and Eve" picture from "The Drama Begins," eyedropper, and food coloring.

When God created the world, it was perfect. Everything was beautiful and worked in order. If you had been there, you would have been amazed at how wonderful everything was.

Adam and Eve lived in a garden where God had placed them. **Hold up the picture of "Adam and Eve."** They worked tending the garden and enjoyed each other's company.

God had put two special trees in the garden. **Read Genesis 2:8,9.** God gave Adam instructions about the trees. **Read Genesis 2:16,17.** Those instructions were not hard to obey, but disobeying them would cause bad consequences.

Adam and Eve enjoyed being with God. Their lives were full of good things. But that wasn't enough for them.

Read Genesis 3:1–7. When Adam and Eve chose to disobey God, sin entered the world.

- How would you describe Satan's personality when he appeared as a serpent to Adam and Eve? *(He was sneaky. He lied. He didn't tell the whole truth. He wanted them to go against God.)*

- Do you think Satan and his evil forces use the same tactics today? How does he do it? *(Yes, he tries to get people to go against God. He makes sin look fun. He doesn't tell the whole truth about what sin will do when you commit the sin.)*

- Whose word did Satan question when he tempted Eve to sin? *(God's.)*

- Why was it wrong for Adam and Eve to eat of this tree? *(Because God had told them not to.)*

There is an interesting verse in the New Testament that describes the different ways that Satan tempts people to sin. **Read 1 John 2:16.** There are three kinds of temptations that Satan uses: 1) Our cravings; 2) The things we see that create bad desires; 3) Our boasting and pride. In fact, just as he tempted Eve, Satan used those same three kinds of temptations when he tempted Jesus in the wilderness.

1. Our cravings—Satan tried to talk Jesus into turning stones into bread when Jesus was hungry. Hunger is a craving. Being hungry is not wrong unless you satisfy your craving in a wrong way. If Jesus had done what Satan suggested, He would have done something wrong. Today, stealing a cookie from the kitchen when your mother says "no cookies" would be satisfying a craving in a sinful way.

2. Bad desires—Satan promised to give Jesus all the kingdoms of the world if Jesus would bow down to him. Wanting to be in charge of something so badly that you get it the wrong way is a bad desire. Jesus deserved to rule the world. He is God. But if He bowed down to Satan, He would have sinned. But He did not! Today, wanting to be class president so badly that you give your classmates gifts to vote for you would be sinning so you could become someone important.

3. Pride and boasting—Satan took Jesus to the top of the temple and told Him to throw Himself off so the angels would catch Him and save Him. If Jesus had tested God to see if He would have done something special to save His Son, that would have been prideful and full of boasting. Jesus didn't need to prove that God would take care of Him. He knew that for sure. He refused to listen to Satan. Today, getting a perfect score on a test, then bragging about your good grade to make sure other people know how smart you are would be sinning.

When Adam and Eve sinned, it put a dark mark on the world. Imagine that God's creation was like this white paper towel. **Bring out the paper towels on the cookie sheet or board.** See how pure this towel is. There are no marks or blemishes on it. But then Adam and Eve sinned. **Using the eyedropper, have a student place one drop of food coloring in the middle of the towel. The drop will spread.**

Do you notice that the drop spread? It didn't stay in a neat little circle, did it? That's the way sin is. It always spreads. That's why Adam and Eve sewed clothes out of leaves for themselves. Their sin made them look at themselves differently. Suddenly, they decided they needed to be covered. Sin always makes a change in the way we think.

But that wasn't all. Their sin kept spreading. **Read Genesis 3:8–10.** Did you notice that Adam sinned again? He lied to God. That wasn't very smart because God already knew about all that Adam and Eve had done. **Have a student place a second drop onto the paper towels in another place.**

Do you think that was the end of it? Not a chance. **Read Genesis 3:11,12.** Now Adam tried to blame Eve for what he had done. That was another sin. **Have a student add another drop in another place on the towels.**

The sin kept spreading. **Read Genesis 3:13.** Now Eve blames her sin on the serpent. It seems that no one was willing to take responsibility. **Have another student place another drop on the towels.**

You can see how the first sin led to many others. Sin was spreading throughout the world. **Hold up the paper towels.**

- How does this activity show how bad sin really is? (*Sin just keeps spreading. If you sin once, you'll sin again to cover up the first time. Sin always looks ugly.*)

What did God think about sin in His perfect world? It did not please Him at all. These sins were very serious in God's eyes. He had to punish those who had sinned. **Read Genesis 3:14–19.** The saddest part of this true story is that Adam and Eve's sin started a sin pattern that has continued throughout history. Today, you sin and I sin. Everyone sins. And we all deserve a punishment of eternal death for the sins we have committed.

Perhaps you think that the story of Adam and Eve is totally depressing. It's not! This is when God first made His promise to send Jesus to save the people. **Read Genesis 3:15.** In the original language in which this verse was written, the "offspring" of the woman means a child who has no human father. There is only one Person on earth who did not have a biological father—and that is Jesus. He had only a biological mother—Mary.

This verse says that Jesus will come and that He will crush the head of the serpent (Satan). And Satan will strike the heel of this Person. Satan did strike at Jesus when he made sure Jesus was crucified on a cross. But Jesus crushed Satan when He rose from the dead and gained victory over sin and death forever! When Jesus comes back to earth to reign as King of kings and Lord of lords, He will totally crush Satan for all of eternity!

Aren't you glad that you have become part of God's family by receiving Jesus as your Savior through prayer?

> *Optional Activity:* This would be a good time to present the way to receive Christ to your class if you have students who are not believers. To help you present this essential biblical truth, use the children's tract *Would You Like to Belong to God's Family?* to lead your students to Christ. See ordering information in the Resources at the back of the book.

God was also looking out for the people He had created. Now that there was sin, the world would be different. It wouldn't be the perfect garden Adam and Eve had lived in before. God was sending them out into the world because they could no longer live in the garden. **Read Genesis 3:20–24.**

As we read, Adam and Eve's sin affected not just them, but the entire world. **Read Romans 5:12.**

- How does Adam and Eve's sin affect us today? (*The world is still cursed. Their sin spread to me so I am a sinner too. I was under a sentence of death for my sin before Jesus saved me.*)

- Name a kind of sin and how it might affect you today. (*Allow students to answer. Examples include:*)

(*Craving—I want something so much that I steal it.*)

(*Bad desires—I want to be popular, so I say mean things about other kids so other people won't like them.*)

(Pride or boasting—I think I am the greatest at baseball, so I look down on my friend who isn't as good as I am.)

So this is a story of bad news and good news. The bad news is that Adam and Eve fell into sin. The good news is that God had a plan for sin—sending His Son Jesus to die and pay the penalty for our sin!

LESSON ACTIVITY: Watch It Grow

> 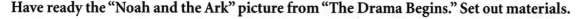 *Teaching Tip:* You can choose to break into smaller groups to do this activity. If so, you will need multiple sets of supplies. You can make the activity into a contest to see which group can make the tallest mountain.

Have ready the "Noah and the Ark" picture from "The Drama Begins." Set out materials.

Take a look at this can. **Hold up the can of shaving cream or Silly String.** How tall is this can?

Let students estimate the height, then measure the can and announce the measured height. We are going to build a mountain with the contents of the can. Let's see how tall our mountain will be. **When finished creating the mountain, say:** Let's measure our mountain's height. **Have a student measure the shaving cream or Silly String mountain. Compare the mountain height to the height of the can. Then say:** There is quite a difference. It's hard to believe that all of that mountain once fit into that little can.

- Can we put all of this material back into the can? Why or why not? *(No, because once it's out, it's too big and messy to put back in. No, because it has changed so it won't fit anymore.)*

Once the material is released from the can, it is impossible to put it back in.

In our Bible lesson today, we learned that sin came into the world through Adam and Eve. Just like the contents of this can, we found out that the act committed by Adam and Eve couldn't be put back or undone. One sin led to another. Sin kept multiplying until it was totally out of control. Adam and Eve's one act allowed sin to spread all over the earth.

The Bible doesn't tell us the kind of sin Adam and Eve committed next, but we know that, just like us, they kept on doing wrong things. Their sin kept building up. The Bible does tell us that they had two boys named Cain and Abel. Cain eventually murdered Abel. This was the first time the sin of murder was committed in the world!

As time went on, the earth became more evil. By the time a man named Noah lived on earth, God saw how wicked mankind had become. It made God sorry that He had created people. He decided to wipe mankind from the face of the earth through a flood. But He also noticed Noah's actions. This is what the Bible says about Noah. **Read Genesis 6:9.**

God told Noah this: **Read Genesis 6:12–14.** God told Noah to build an ark and bring two animals of every kind and put them on the ark. After Noah and his family were on board, God shut the door and it started to rain. **Hold up the picture of "Noah and the Ark."**

The great flood covered the whole earth. All the people and animals on the earth were destroyed except for those in the ark.

Many months after he entered the ark, Noah led his family back out onto dry ground. The flood was over! Then God sent Noah a rainbow as a promise that He would never cause a flood to destroy the earth again.

Remember how we learned that Jesus is the central Person in the Bible? Some Bible teachers explain that the story of Noah and the ark is a picture of how Christians are saved from God's punishment. The people who went into the ark trusted in God, and God saved them from destruction. Jesus is like the ark. When we are "safe" in Jesus, we will not face God's punishment for our sins. Jesus is our protection.

- If you had lived during the time of Noah, do you think you would have gotten on the ark? Why or why not? (*Yes, because I believe what God says. Maybe I would have listened to the people around me instead of Noah.*)

- Why do you think God chose Noah to build the ark? (*Because Noah listened to God. Noah loved God and obeyed Him.*)

- What does this show us about obeying God? (*We need to obey even if we don't understand why. We shouldn't let other people talk us into doing what is wrong.*)

- What happens when we do obey God? (*Things turn out right. We please God.*)

APPLICATION: Obedience and Disobedience

Have ready the picture of "Abraham and Isaac."

Abraham is one of the most well known people in history. Because of Abraham's great faith, he received many promises that came true over thousands of years. One of the promises was that the whole world would be blessed through him and his son, Isaac.

- Why do your teachers give you tests in your classes? (*To make sure we know what we studied. To help us remember what we know.*)

God gave Abraham a different kind of test—a test of his obedience and faith. Do you remember how people worshiped God in the Old Testament? They took a lamb to an altar of stones and killed it as an offering for sin. The killing of the lamb was a picture of how Jesus was to come and be killed on the cross to pay for our sins. (Jesus is called the Lamb of God.)

But in Genesis 22, we read about how God told Abraham to take his beloved son Isaac up to a mountain, tie him up, and offer him on an altar.

- How do you think Abraham reacted to this command? (*He obeyed right away. He wondered what God was doing. He argued with God.*)

The next morning, Abraham did as he was told without arguing or hesitating. He brought enough wood to make a fire. It took Abraham three days to walk to the mountain where God told him to go. He left his servants at the bottom of the mountain, and he and

Isaac walked up to the top. Isaac carried the wood for the fire; Abraham carried the fire and the knife.

Along the way, Isaac asked his father, "The fire and the wood are here, but where is the lamb for the burnt offering?"

Abraham answered, "God Himself will provide the lamb." Abraham had faith in God to provide.

Hold up the picture of Abraham's sacrifice. When they came to the right place, Abraham built the altar, put the wood on top, and tied up his son. Can you imagine how he was feeling? Then he took out the knife and raised it to kill Isaac. Just then, God said, "Abraham, don't hurt the boy. Now I know that you love me more than even your own son."

Abraham looked to one side, and there, caught in the bushes, was a ram—an animal that God provided for the sacrifice. That's what Abraham used as an offering to the Lord.

Because Abraham trusted God so completely, God gave him this promise. **Read Genesis 22:15–18.**

So far in this lesson, we've learned that:

- Adam and Eve disobeyed God and sin entered the world.

- Cain disobeyed God and the first murder was committed.

- Noah obeyed God and his whole family was saved from the worldwide flood.

- Abraham obeyed God and his actions blessed the whole world.

Have students form groups of no more than four. In your group, discuss what you think is the most important thing about obedience or disobedience that you should remember to do in your daily life. An example would be to say no when someone asks you to do something that's not right.

Give groups a few minutes to discuss. Then have groups report the one most important thing they decided on. Write their ideas on the board.

These are all essential things we must remember to do. Obeying God is so important. This week, put into practice one of the ideas we have written on the board. See if you can be more obedient to God this next week.

CHECK FOR UNDERSTANDING: Old Testament Time Line

Before Class: On a large piece of butcher paper (approximately 7 feet long), create a time line by drawing a long horizontal line across the paper. On the left end, draw a vertical line and label it "Creation." On the right end, draw a vertical line with a manger near it (signifying the birth of Jesus) to mark the end of the Old Testament times. Label the time line "Old Testament Times." You will be taping drawings of biblical events to the time line.

For the next four lessons, the students will be assembling an Old Testament time line. Each week, you will add several drawings. Use tape or sticky tack to attach the drawings to the time line.

Gather the pictures that you cut apart from "The Drama Begins." This lesson, we are going to start a new project. We will make a time line of the Old Testament times. During each lesson, we will add drawings of the people and events we study.

This line (**point to the first vertical line**) represents the beginning of time. This line (**point to the last vertical line**) with the manger refers to the birth of Jesus Christ. That is when the Old Testament times ended.

Show the four pictures and tape them to the time line in appropriate places, identifying the subject of the pictures as you do.

Now remove the pictures and mix them up. Have four volunteers come up one at a time, select a picture, tell who it is, and tape it at the right place on the line.

MEMORY VERSE ACTIVITY: Verse Pairs

Romans 5:12—"Therefore, just as sin entered the world through one man, and death through sin, and in this way death came to all men, because all sinned."

Write the verse on the board. Divide students into pairs and assign each pair a number. Instruct pairs to memorize the verse together.

When pairs finish, have all students sit in a circle next to their partners. Call out a number. One person in that pair must say the verse when their number is called. If a number is called more than once, the second person must recite the verse. The partner can give two helps. If a student cannot recite the verse, the pair leaves the circle.

See which pair remains the longest. Then say the verse together as a class and compliment all the pairs for their hard work.

WEEKLY ASSIGNMENT: Order Please

This week students will begin memorizing the names of the Minor Prophets: Hosea, Joel, Amos, Obadiah, Jonah, Micah, Nahum, Habakkuk, Zephaniah, Haggai, Zechariah, and Malachi.

Have students record their daily reading assignments in their journals:

Day 1—Hosea 11
Day 2—Joel 1
Day 3—Jonah 1
Day 4—Jonah 2
Day 5—Jonah 3
Day 6—Jonah 4
Day 7—Micah 7

To help you become familiar with the Old Testament, you have been memorizing the names of the books in order. In this lesson, we will work on the last group of books, the Minor Prophets.

Knowing the order of the books of the Bible helps when you are looking up verses. You can then locate these verses without looking at the Contents page. **Pass out the "Order Please" handouts.** This is a list of the books in the Old Testament. They give much of the early history of the world and contain some wonderful poetry and numerous accurate prophecies. You can memorize the order of these books in any way you choose. A game idea has been included on the handout. You can choose to memorize the books of the Bible by playing this game.

Read the directions for the game on the handout. Play a round of the game if you have time.

Close in prayer, praising God for creating the world and for having a plan to send His Son, Jesus.

The Drama Begins

Creation

Abraham offering Isaac

Adam and Eve and the serpent in the garden

Noah and the ark

Order Please!

Make a chart on a chalkboard or poster board that has numbers from 1 to 39. Number on the back of the squares from 1 to 39 so that Genesis is 1, Exodus is 2, Leviticus is 3, etc. Cut apart the squares. Leave the squares face up so that the Bible books can be seen but the numbers are hidden. Play with a family member to see if you can put the books in order. Take turns choosing a book square and taping it beside a number. If the number matches, the person gets a point. The person with the most points wins.

Genesis	Exodus	Leviticus	Numbers
Deuteronomy	Joshua	Judges	Ruth
1 Samuel	2 Samuel	1 Kings	2 Kings
1 Chronicles	2 Chronicles	Ezra	Nehemiah
Esther	Job	Psalms	Proverbs
Ecclesiastes	Song of Solomon	Isaiah	Jeremiah
Lamentations	Ezekiel	Daniel	Hosea
Joel	Amos	Obadiah	Jonah
Micah	Nahum	Habakkuk	Zephaniah
Haggai	Zechariah	Malachi	

LESSON 6

Law and Grace

LESSON PLAN

OBJECTIVE: Students will understand our inability to keep the law and our need for God's grace.

APPLICATION: Students will commit themselves to practicing the Law of Love in the classroom.

LESSON PLAN ELEMENT	ACTIVITY	TIME	SUPPLIES
Opening Activity	*Follow the Leader*	7–10	Bible
Bible Story—Genesis 12–14, the Passover and the Exodus	*Lessons from the Past*	10–15	Bible; dry-erase marker or chalk; 1 copy of "The Passover" master; scissors
Lesson Activity	*How to Win the Prize*	7–10	Bible; candy prize for each student; paper; pencils; 1 copy of "The Ten Commandments" master (enlarge if possible); yardstick
Application	*The Love Law*	7–10	Bible; newsprint or butcher paper; black marker; masking tape
Check for Understanding	*Following the Time Line*	3–5	All the pictures used so far in previous time line activities (You might want to recopy pictures so that your time line remains intact); tape
Memory Verse Activity	*Lead Me to It*	3–5	Blindfold; 6 index cards; pen; dry-erase marker or chalk
Weekly Assignment	*Law and Grace*	3–5	

So far, your students have heard about the events of creation, the Fall of humankind, Noah and his ark, and Abraham's willingness to sacrifice his son, Isaac, before the Lord. Abraham's line, through Isaac, led to the nation of Israel. Through Abraham, God would bless the world by sending His Son, Jesus, to save all who turn to Him. As God had promised when Adam first sinned, He had a plan to bring men and women to Him.

Jacob, the grandson of Abraham, took his family to Egypt to escape a famine. After four hundred years, his descendants had multiplied greatly. When a new king of Egypt arose who was concerned about their numbers, he subjected the Israelites to cruel slavery.

Exodus 1 and 2 give an account of this development, of the birth and life of Moses, and of the people's cry to God for deliverance. God heard their cry and sent Moses to lead them out of Egypt.

The people of Israel were on their way to the land God promised to give them. On the way, they crossed a wilderness. While there, Moses went up to the top of Mount Sinai and received the Ten Commandments. They are the central principles of the complete Law that Moses received that set up the religious and governmental structure for the national life of Israel.

In God's holy Word, the Law of Moses and God's grace are constantly set in contrast. Under the Law, God demanded righteousness *from* man. The Law was connected with works. Under grace, God in Christ gives righteousness *to* man, and that righteousness becomes ours by faith (John 1:17; Ephesians 2:8,9).

By the Law we have knowledge of sin (Romans 3:20; 7:7; Galatians 3:19). Paul writes, "I felt fine so long as I did not understand what the law really demanded. But when I learned the truth, I realized that I had broken the law and was a sinner, doomed to die" (Romans 7:9, TLB).

Paul laments that, because of his sinful nature, he constantly struggles with wrongdoing. "I love to do God's will so far as my new nature is concerned; but there is something else deep within me, in my lower nature, that is at war with my mind and wins the fight and makes me a slave to the sin that is still within me . . . Oh, what a terrible predicament I'm in. Who will free me from my slavery to this deadly lower nature?" (Romans 7:22–25, TLB).

This is the struggle of every child of God apart from His grace. Jesus Christ delivers us from the guilt imposed by the Law and the bondage created by our sins. Yet we are still hindered by our sinful nature. Your students are in this battle just as you are. But Paul writes, "Thank God! It has been done by Jesus Christ our Lord. He has set me free" (verse 25, TLB). How much more can we give children than showing them the joy and freedom they have in the grace they have received?

While Jesus presents the ultimate portrait of God's grace, we can also see a full gallery of His mercy in the stories of the Old Testament. It is evident from the struggles of man under the Law that deliverance could come only by God's mercy and grace. Thus we have a balance between God's judgment of sin and His means of restoration for those who truly trust and obey Him.

Is your classroom a place of grace? Are you modeling Christ's unconditional love in the way you direct your students? A classroom has rules that all must follow. But the rules are not the greatest learning tools. Instead, the deep love of a teacher who recognizes each person's failings, insecurities, and inadequacies—and yet accepts that person as he or she is—will teach students the kind of acceptance and care that only Christ can give. Make it your prayer to reach your students' hearts with the love of Christ and His grace within the structure of your classroom discipline. Your example will bring this lesson to the hearts of your students much more than any activity can.

DING! DONG!

LESSON PLAN

OPENING ACTIVITY: Follow the Leader

Before Class: Identify areas in the building that your class can visit, such as other rooms or classrooms. If possible, make prior arrangements to barge into a room and interrupt what's going on.

Discuss how playing the "Order Please" game helped your students become familiar with and memorize the books of the Bible. Find out how students are doing on their memorization. Offer to help those who are struggling.

Today, I want to take you on a tour of our building. I want you to get an idea of all the different areas and things we have in our building. It is very important for you to listen to me and follow me closely so that we don't disturb others in the building.

On your tour, use various examples of poor leadership. As you lead the class around the building, point to areas or things and call them by the wrong names. Get mixed up and retrace your steps. Stop suddenly so that the students bump into each other. At times, speak too loudly and then too softly. Allow one or two children to go into a room to look, but no one else. If you have made prior arrangements, barge in and interrupt another class. When your class is frustrated, bring the students back to your classroom.

- How would you describe me as a leader today? (*Confused, rude, didn't know what you were doing.*)

Explain that you were not a good leader and discuss all the things that you did wrong, such as not having a thought-out plan and not being familiar with many things.

Having a good leader is important. God used a man who displayed good leadership in the beginning of the Old Testament. His name was Moses. But Moses didn't start out his life acting like he would be a great leader. He was raised in a palace but he ended up fleeing for his life because he murdered someone. He spent forty years living in the desert. Even though Moses did not look like a great leader, he had something that God knew would eventually help him become a great leader. **Read Hebrews 11:24–27.**

- What leadership quality did Moses have? (*Faith.*)

God told Moses to go back to Egypt and tell the Israelites about God's plan to free them and to ask the elders to go with Moses to demand that the Pharaoh free the people. This was Moses' response. **Read Exodus 4:1.** The Lord then showed Moses three miracles to prove that God was behind him. Let's read what his excuse was then. **Read Exodus 4:10.** The Lord was not pleased with this excuse, so he assigned Moses' brother, Aaron, to be his spokesman.

- Why do you think Moses was so afraid to speak for God? (*He didn't want to face Pharaoh. He thought he couldn't do a good job.*)

- How is this like times when you know God wants you to do something difficult? (*I sometimes feel I can't do a good job. Sometimes it's hard to do what God says because other people make fun of me or don't understand what I'm doing.*)

After all his excuses, Moses went to do what God said. Let's hear about that in our Bible Story.

BIBLE STORY: Lessons from the Past

 Before Class: Cut apart the three pictures on the "Passover" reproducible.

Moses was one of the greatest leaders of all time. He loved God; he obeyed God; and he was patient with the Israelites. Even today, the Jewish people and Christians honor the memory of Moses and all he did.

We learned about how Moses was chosen by God to lead the people. When he went down into Egypt, he was taking his life in his hands. He didn't know if the Pharaoh would kill him or not. But he trusted God to keep him safe so he could do the job God had sent him to do.

Moses had one command for the Pharaoh: "Let God's people go."

Pharaoh did not want to let the people go because he needed them as slaves to build the great monuments in Egypt. He wanted the cheap labor. So Pharaoh wouldn't listen to God. Moses kept performing the miracles God told him to do to change Pharaoh's mind, but Pharaoh still wouldn't listen.

- Moses turned the Egyptians' water—rivers, lakes, streams, even buckets of water—into blood. All the fish died and everything stank.

- Moses made frogs come up from the Nile River and these frogs got into every home and covered the land. Then at Moses' command all the frogs died.

- Moses made gnats, or small biting insects, come from the dust of the land. They were on all the people and all the animals.

- Moses caused flies to swarm throughout Egypt and into Pharaoh's palace.

- Moses caused all the livestock (farm animals) of the Egyptians to get sick and die. The livestock that belonged to the people of Israel did not get sick.

- Moses caused boils (huge, painful sores) to cover the people and animals of Egypt.

- Moses caused hail to fall from the sky. Moses warned the people to bring inside everything that could get harmed. Those who believed in God did that, but those who did not believe God ignored what Moses said and their slaves and animals were killed. But there was no hail where the Israelites lived.

- Moses caused a wind to blow that carried locusts, or huge grasshoppers, over the land. The locusts invaded all the homes of the Egyptians and destroyed all their crops.

- Moses caused darkness to spread over Egypt for three days.

- Last, Moses caused the oldest son of every family in Egypt to die.

These plagues took place one right after another, just days apart. When Moses would warn Pharaoh to let the people go, Pharaoh would say he would, but then he would harden his heart and say no. Then the plague would come. Pharaoh would call out to Moses to take away the plague and lead the people out. But as soon as Moses took away the plague, Pharaoh would change his mind again.

Before the last plague, when the oldest son of each family died, God asked the people of Israel to do something to prove that they loved and obeyed God. He said, "Take the best lamb of your flock, slaughter it, and take some of the blood to put on the sides and tops of the doorframes of your houses. That night, have everything packed and ready to go. Have a last meal where you eat the meat of the lamb, but eat it with your coat and your sandals on and everything ready to go."

This meal was called the Passover. That was a reminder to the Israelites that at midnight, death passed over each house that was marked with blood and no one died in that house. But the Egyptian people woke to find the oldest son in each family had died.

Then Pharaoh summoned Moses and told him to take the Israelite people and leave. **Read Exodus 12:31–36.** The people were ready to go. They had their things packed, their coats and sandals on, and they had eaten. When Moses gave the order, they all left. Millions of Hebrew people went. Can you imagine what that looked like? The amazing part of this story is that the Egyptians were so anxious for the people to leave that they gave the Israelites lots of gold, silver, and other valuables to take with them. In God's eyes, this was payment for all the years that the Israelites had worked as slaves and not been paid for all their hard labor.

Hold up the picture of the Passover.

Let's look at the directions that God gave to the Israelites for the Passover and see how it is a picture of Jesus.

Write these column headings on the board: "Passover" and "What it means." Read the following verses and write the idea in the "Passover" column. Discuss what it means, emphasizing the verse and idea from the "What it means" column.

PASSOVER	WHAT IT MEANS
1. Each family picked out a lamb (Exodus 12:3).	Jesus is the Lamb of God (John 1:29).
2. The animal had to be perfect (Exodus 12:5).	Jesus was perfect, without sin (1 Peter 2:22).
3. The family sacrificed the lamb (Exodus 12:6).	Jesus was sacrificed for our sins (1 Corinthians 5:7).

PASSOVER	WHAT IT MEANS
4. They put blood on the doorposts at the top and sides. Those who were protected by the shed blood were not destroyed (Exodus 12:7,13).	Jesus died on the cross for us and His blood was the payment for our sin (Hebrews 9:12,14).
5. The people who refused to put blood on their doorposts had someone in their family die (Exodus 12:29,20).	If we reject the blood of Jesus, we will die in our sins (Romans 3:25).

Here is an amazing sign. **On the board, draw a doorpost like the one in the "Passover" picture. Put "blood smears" on the top center and on each side of the doorpost. Draw a line from the blood smear on one side of the doorpost to the other. Then draw a line straight down from the top smear of blood. The lines will form a cross.** Do you see what this shows? A cross.

That night, the Israelite people were allowed to leave Egypt. But then Pharaoh changed his mind again. He sent his entire army after the Israelites to bring them back. Because the people of Israel had their animals, their children, their elderly, and all their belongings, the soldiers could travel much faster than they could. The people soon came to the Red Sea. Of course, they had no boats to cross, and the soldiers were coming up behind them fast.

Moses said to the people, "Don't be afraid! God will deliver you from these soldiers."

I'm sure you've heard the story. Moses put his staff into the water, and the Red Sea parted. There was dry land between the walls of water! The people and all their animals crossed the Red Sea in safety. **Show the picture of the people crossing the Red Sea.**

The soldiers came in after them! But God protected His people. The wheels fell off the Egyptians' chariots so they couldn't drive. The soldiers became afraid and confused. **Read Exodus 14:25.** As soon as all the Israelite people were across, God told Moses to stretch out his hand over the water. The Red Sea went back into its place. **Read Exodus 14:27,28.**

Write these columns on the board, read the verses, and discuss the material.

WHAT HAPPENED	WHAT IT MEANS
1. God promised to bring the people to a wonderful land of richness (Exodus 3:7,8).	God promises that as His children, we will live rich, abundant lives (John 10:10).
2. God protected the people when they obeyed Him (Exodus 14:29–31).	God protects us as believers (Psalm 125:2).

Looking at these stories in the Old Testament, we can see that God doesn't change. He keeps watch over His people and leads them in the way they should go.

LESSON ACTIVITY: How to Win the Prize

Before Class: Buy candy prizes that your students will really enjoy, such as large candy bars. Make sure you have a prize for each student.

Bring out half the prizes you brought. (Keep the other half hidden so it looks like only some students will win prizes.) Divide your class into two groups, and give each group a piece of paper and a pencil. Assign one person in each group as the scribe to write the rules.

Give these rules. They are so strict that there is little possibility that anyone can fulfill them. That is the purpose of the activity. I am going to give your group two minutes to write the Ten Commandments as they are written in Exodus 20:3–17. They must be word-perfect and in order. You cannot look in your Bible. If you win, each person in your group will receive one of these prizes. **Point out the prizes.**

Say "go" and let groups work. After two minutes, call time. Then check to see if the rules were followed perfectly.

I'm sorry, but neither group won this race. Both groups lost so you do not deserve to get a prize. **Set the prizes aside, but leave them out so the students can see them.**

- What was there about this contest that you didn't like? *(It was too hard. I knew I couldn't win no matter how hard I tried.)*

- How did it feel when neither group won? *(The contest was unfair. I couldn't believe it.)*

- The Bible has lots of rules. How does it feel to have to obey all these rules perfectly all the time? *(Sometimes I get discouraged. It doesn't seem fair.)*

When the children of Israel were traveling through the wilderness, they came to Mount Sinai. They stopped there to rest awhile. God told Moses to come up to the top of the mountain to receive the Ten Commandments. These rules are the center of God's Law.

Tape up "The Ten Commandments" poster. These are the Ten Commandments. **Read them through with your students. Explain any that your students may not understand.**

God says that anyone who breaks one of these laws deserves punishment. Let's be honest:

- How many of these commandments have you broken in your lifetime? *(Allow students time to count and respond.)*

If we are honest, we have to admit that we break at least one of these Ten Commandments every day. In fact, it is impossible to keep the Ten Commandments. The only Person who ever kept them all was Jesus, and He is God.

Hold up the yardstick. This yardstick measures how long something is. In an amusement park, some rides have a yardstick to measure a rider's height. If you aren't tall enough, you cannot go on the ride. That's the way God's Law is. It measures our righteousness. If we can't measure up by obeying all of God's Law all the time, we won't be able to go to heaven and be with God. If you come up short, you can't go. As you can see, we all fall short of God's yardstick, the Ten Commandments. We can never take that "ride" to heaven.

But the Bible teaches about something that is the opposite of Law. That is grace. Grace means receiving something good that we don't deserve. God sent His Son, Jesus, to earth to take the punishment for our sins and to end all God's anger against us. We didn't deserve that. God did it because He loves us, not because we are so wonderful. That is God's grace.

God used the blood of Jesus and our faith as the way of saving us from punishment. In this way, God could be entirely fair and still be entirely holy. In His holiness, He cannot let any sinfulness into heaven. But in His love, He doesn't want anyone to go into eternal punishment. So Jesus came to take our punishment, and God offers us the free gift of eternal life when we believe in Jesus.

- How does trying to keep the strict Law make you feel? *(Like I am never going to be good enough. Like a failure.)*

- How does knowing about God's grace make you feel? *(Like God really loves me. Like I can really make it to heaven even though I'm not perfect and I can't keep God's Law perfectly.)*

- How would you explain the difference between Law and grace to someone who is trying to get to heaven by being good enough? *(I would say that we can never be good enough and that we need God's grace to get there. I would tell that person that no one can keep God's Law; we all break the Ten Commandments, and because Jesus died for our sins we can ask God to forgive us.)*

Here is the interesting thing about Law and grace in the Bible. Jesus is the central part of both. **Read Matthew 5:17,18.** Jesus fulfilled the Law by keeping every bit of it.

- How was our contest to write the Ten Commandments like trying to keep all of God's laws? *(There was no way we could win the prize and there's no way we can keep God's laws.)*

Guess what? The rules kept you from winning the prizes I had for you. But now I am going to give you the prizes anyway. **Take out the prizes you had hidden and the ones that are in plain view and give each student a prize.** I am giving you these prizes even though you didn't deserve them. That's what grace is.

- How does it feel to receive grace rather than law? *(It's exciting. It makes me happy.)*

APPLICATION: The Law of Love

I didn't have to sacrifice much to give you these prizes in our Lesson Activity, just a few dollars. But God had to sacrifice His Son on the cross to give us His grace, which is His forgiveness. In other words, when we can't follow God's Law without failure, when we break one of His commands, in His grace He forgives us of our sins when we ask.

Jesus told His disciples how we can fulfill the Law in the best way. **Read Mark 12:29–31.** God gave us two rules that sum up all the other rules:

1. Love God with all your heart, soul, mind, and strength.

2. Love your neighbor just as much as you love yourself.

We can think of God's Law and His grace, all wrapped up together, as the Law of Love. We love God because He loves us. We love others because God wants us to love them. Let's see if we can brainstorm ways that we can practice the Law of Love. First, let's start with loving God.

Discuss ways each person could show love for God. Write these ways on the newsprint or butcher paper. Some examples could be: praise God for being so loving; thank God for all the good things He has given us; talk to God many times a day; read God's love letter to us, the Bible. Help your students come up with other suggestions.

Now let's see if we can come up with some ideas for practicing the second part of the Law of Love, loving each other. **Help students come up with ideas on how they could treat each other with love. Some examples could be: greet each person as he or she arrives; don't have favorites but treat everyone equally; don't call people names; compliment people on what they do well; smile at each other; pray for each other. Help your students come up with other suggestions, especially ones that deal with personality problems in your classroom.**

Post the list in your classroom. Each day when you come into the room, remind yourself of these rules. Let's see if we can improve on the ways we practice the Law of Love in our classroom.

As the lessons continue in this series, keep emphasizing the Law of Love suggestions and commend your students when you see them practicing them. You could add to these suggestions as needed.

CHECK FOR UNDERSTANDING: Following the Time Line

Before Class: Select some sentences from the activities in lessons 5 and 6 that tell facts about each of the pictures from "The Drama Begins" and "The Passover." Write the sentences out so that you can read them during this activity.

As we have been learning about the history of the Old Testament, we have been placing pictures on a time line. Today, we are going to play a game to help us remember the correct order of the historical events we have studied so far. **Have seven volunteers come to the front of the class. Tape one of the pictures to each person's chest or abdomen. (Do not have students stand in the correct order.) Have them choose an action they can do such as wiggle their fingers, jump up and down, wave, bend and touch their toes.**

 Teaching Tip: Cover your time line so that students are doing this activity from memory.

GROWING IN GOD'S WORD

I will read a statement that we have learned about one of the pictures shown. Each person in front will be doing a chosen action. Decide which person's picture that statement is about, then do the same action that person is doing.

Read one of the sentences you selected from Lessons 5 and 6. (Do not read the sentences in chronological order. Mix them up.) Give students time to follow the action of the person they think has the right picture. Check to see how many of the students were correct. Then go on to the next statement.

When finished with the activity, add the three pictures from the "Passover" to your time line.

MEMORY VERSE ACTIVITY: Lead Me to It

    1   *2*   *3*   *4*   *5*   *6*

Romans 6:23—"For the wages / of sin is death, / but the gift of God / is eternal life / in Christ Jesus our Lord."

Before Class: Write the numbers 1 to 6 on the back of index cards and write the verse portions on the other side, matching the numbers with the right verse portion. Split the verse as shown.

While you write the verse on the board, have a student hide the six index cards around the room. Read the verse with your class several times, then say: This verse tells us that we deserve death because of the sins we have committed. But Jesus Christ died on the cross to pay for our sins, giving us the gift of eternal life.

We learned in our lesson today that Moses was a good leader. We are going to practice this verse by playing a leadership game. Our memory verse today is written on several index cards. I am going to blindfold someone and have that person follow directions to find parts of the verse.

Blindfold a volunteer, and spin the person around once or twice. Make sure you know where the first card is. Then give the blindfolded student directions such as "walk two steps forward," "walk three steps to the right," "bend down and pick up the card," and so on.

Have the student take off the blindfold and read the verse portion aloud. Instruct the first student to remain standing while a second student is blindfolded. Have a third student give directions to find the second portion of the verse. (Once the second student is blindfolded, make sure the student giving directions knows where the card is hidden.) Then have the students read each portion in order. Repeat until each part is found.

Hide the index cards again and choose other students to find the verse parts. When the leadership game is finished, have the students say the verse to you individually.

WEEKLY ASSIGNMENT: Law and Grace

This week, have students continue to work on memorizing the names of the Minor Prophets.

Have students record the following daily reading assignments in their journals:

Day 1—Habakkuk 3

Day 2—Haggai 1 and 2

Day 3—Zechariah 1

Day 4—Zechariah 2

Day 5—Zechariah 3

Day 6—Zechariah 4

Day 7—Malachi 3 and 4

Tell your students, This week, look for some examples of law and grace. You could search your newspaper to find stories of a law that has been broken or a new law that has been made. You might find a story about someone who was arrested but was allowed to go free, or a person who was given something for nothing. You might find an example at home, such as having to obey the house rules or having your mom or dad bestow grace on you. Be ready to share about these examples next time.

Close in prayer, asking God to help you and your students to treat others with the Law of Love.

The Passover

The Passover

Moses receiving the Ten Commandments

The Parting of the Red Sea

The Ten Commandments

1. You shall have no other gods.

2. You shall not make for yourself an idol...You shall not bow down to them or worship them.

3. You shall not misuse the name of the Lord.

4. Remember the Sabbath by keeping it holy.

5. Honor your father and mother.

6. You shall not murder.

7. You shall not commit adultery.

8. You shall not steal.

9. You shall not give false testimony.

10. You shall not covet...anything that is your neighbor's.

LESSON 7

Joshua and David

LESSON PLAN

OBJECTIVE: Students will learn to believe the promises of God and maintain fellowship with God, unhindered by sin.

APPLICATION: Students will confess their sins and understand that their sin was forgiven.

LESSON PLAN ELEMENT	ACTIVITY	TIME	SUPPLIES
Opening Activity	*Raisin' Raisins*	7–10	1 jar per group; box of raisins; clear soda (e.g., Sprite or 7–Up)
Bible Story—Joshua 1:1–9 and 2 Samuel 12, God delivers His people through Joshua and forgives David of his sin	*Deliverance and Forgiveness*	10–15	Bibles; 1 copy of "Deliverance," "Forgiveness," and "Joshua and David"
Lesson Activity	*Obedience and Courage*	7–10	Bibles; "Deliverance" and "Forgiveness" copies from Bible Story; pencils
Application	*Real "Raisins" to Confess*	7–10	"'Raisins' to Confess" handouts; pencils; scissors
Check for Understanding	*Raisins in a Row*	3–5	Raisins; paper; pencils; basket or box
Memory Verse Activity	*Raisin Relay*	3–5	Brown construction paper; scissors; heavy black marker; masking tape; straws
Weekly Assignment	*Quick Confession*	3–5	"Real 'Raisins' to Confess" handouts

LESSON INTRODUCTION

In this lesson we will be looking at Joshua and David, two men whose confidence in God brought them to the forefront of greatness. Each man has a distinguishing quality for which he is best known.

Joshua, Moses' brilliant military strategist who eventually led Israel into the Promised Land, is characterized as a *deliverer*. Of the twelve spies sent by Moses into Canaan to survey the territory, Joshua and Caleb alone showed complete confidence that God would help Israel conquer the land. Because of their willingness to believe and obey God, Joshua and Caleb were the only two adults who experienced Egyptian slavery and lived to enter the Promised Land. God appointed Joshua to succeed Moses as Israel's leader and deliverer because he was faithful to ask God's direction in the challenges he faced.

David, a shepherd, poet, and soldier who became Israel's greatest king, is best known for the principle of *forgiveness*. An ancestor of Jesus Christ, he is listed in the Hall of Faith in Hebrews 11 and was described by God Himself as "a man after His own heart" (1 Samuel 13:14). Undoubtedly, he was one of the most famous men of the Old Testament. But he had a dark side as well. He committed adultery with Bathsheba, arranged for the murder of her husband, Uriah, and directly disobeyed God in taking a census of the people.

In spite of his failures, David's unchangeable belief in the faithful and forgiving nature of God is a source of encouragement to us today. David was quick to confess his sins sincerely from his heart, and God never held back His forgiveness (Psalm 32:1–5). The lesson we can learn from this example is that, while God may allow us to suffer the consequences of our sins as He did David, we can count on God's loving forgiveness whenever we fail.

Through the principles of deliverance and forgiveness, Joshua's and David's lives illustrate the work of Jesus Christ on behalf of humankind. Jesus would come and deliver His people from their sins by dying on the cross as payment, opening the way for God to forgive us.

LESSON PLAN

OPENING ACTIVITY: Raisin' Raisins

Discuss with your students the examples they found of law and grace. Talk about the differences in results in each example. Discuss how we need laws to keep the peace, but we also need grace to show mercy and love to others.

Read the following story:

Leisha lived in a small town. She loved God and had made Jesus the Lord of her life. She awoke every morning at 6 a.m., and usually hopped out of bed right away. But this morning, she just turned over and went back to sleep. She was so-o-o-o tired. She had stayed up and read a book until midnight even though her mother had told her several times to shut off the light. Before she knew it, her mother was shaking her and telling her she had overslept. She rushed to get ready for school. Unfortunately, her brother was taking his time in the bathroom. She pounded and shouted at the bathroom door. When her brother finally opened the door she said, "Jerk," and went in to get ready.

When she arrived at the breakfast table, her sister was eating the last doughnut. She yelled at her sister and called her names. Just then the bus pulled up. Leisha grabbed her backpack and slid into an empty seat on the bus. As she sat there, she realized how many times she had done wrong things this morning. She closed her eyes and began to confess them to God.

Just like Leisha, we sin everyday. God may allow us to suffer the consequences of our sin, but we can count on His loving forgiveness whenever we fail.

Let's do an activity to help us understand this. **Divide students into groups of three or four. Set out a jar and raisins for each group. Pour soda into each jar until it is about ¾ full.**

Hold up a raisin. Let's say these raisins represent us Christians. The soda in the jar represents our life. Drop the raisin into the jar of soda. **Have each student put one raisin into the jar of soda.**

Notice that your raisin is falling to the bottom. It's too heavy to float, so it sinks.

That's how it is with us when we try to live on our own without the power of Jesus in our lives. We still sin even though we have Jesus as our personal Savior. Sin can bog us down. We sink even though we want to do what's right. No matter how hard we try, we cannot rise above our sins. It's like we are weighed down with all the bad things we do.

The carbonation (the bubbles) in this soda represents God's power. Once we confess our sins, He lifts the burden off us and we are free of sin. Watch as the raisins rise and then drop again. While they are at the bottom, air bubbles collect around them. Then the bubbles carry them up. That's like when we ask God to forgive us for what we have done wrong. He not only forgives us, He restores our spirits and makes us feel good again. His Spirit enables us to do what's right. See how the raisins rise to the top of the jar. **Let the students watch the raisins for a little while. It takes some time for them to rise to the top. Go around the room and comment on how forgiveness makes us feel and how God's power keeps us free from sin.**

- How is the raisin like someone who has a lot of sin in his or her life? (*When the raisin let go of the bubbles, it fell back down to the bottom. When we let go of God's way and choose to sin, our spirits get loaded down.*)

- How do you feel after you realize you have sinned? (*I feel depressed. I know I've done wrong and I wish I could go back and change what I did. I feel badly.*)

- What is one area of your life that you have a hard time controlling and that often leads you to sin? (*My temper, I'm always getting mad. Telling the truth, I usually try to get out of situations by lying. Money, as soon as I get a few dollars I spend it and then don't have anything left for the good stuff I want to do.*)

- Who do you know that is a good example of a person who follows God's way? (*My mom, because she's always thinking about other people first. My dad, because he makes sure we get to church and that we think about Jesus all the time. My grandmother, because she prays a lot and reads her Bible.*)

- What does this person do after recognizing that he or she has sinned? (*My mom sometimes cries after she gets mad at me, then asks me to forgive her. My dad once yelled at my mom and then had to ask her to forgive him.*)

In our Bible Story today, we are going to learn about two men who knew all about God's power and forgiveness. Their experiences are very different and yet their lives show the wonderful nature of God's love toward us.

BIBLE STORY: Deliverance and Forgiveness

 Before Class: Cut apart the two pictures on the "Joshua and David" copy.

God promises to do two things for His children:

1. He promises to deliver them from the power of sin.

2. He promises to forgive them when they sin and ask for His forgiveness.

We will be studying the lives of two Bible characters today. Each person's life demonstrates one of these truths about God and His Son, Jesus.

Divide the class into two groups. In each group, assign a good reader to read and a reporter to tell the group's story. Give each group one of the two reproducible pages for this activity ("Deliverance" for the Joshua group and "Forgiveness" for the David group). Also, give each group the appropriate picture from "Joshua and David."

In your group, your reader will read aloud the story on your worksheet. There are some

Bible references after the story. Skim through the passages and decide what information about your Bible character you want to add to your story. Be prepared to tell the story to the rest of the class.

Give groups five minutes to work. Circulate among the groups, helping them as needed.

When students are finished, have the "Joshua" group give their report first. The reporter will use the "Joshua" picture to tell the story of Joshua. Then have the "David" group follow the same pattern.

Add the "Joshua" and "David" pictures to the time line.

LESSON ACTIVITY: Obedience and Courage

We can say that Joshua shows the Lord's deliverance. Joshua freed the Promised Land from the people living there who were worshiping idols and doing all kinds of wicked things. When the Israelites obeyed God, God gave them victory in battle and their enemies were defeated. When the Israelites disobeyed God, they did not have God's help in battle and were defeated by their enemies.

We can say that David shows God's loving forgiveness. David wanted to follow the Lord. He did many things that were right, even when times were difficult. But he also failed God by committing sin.

When David sinned, he came to God to confess his sins and ask for forgiveness. God always forgave David.

Select one person in each group as a scribe. Make sure the scribes have pencils. Have each group complete the questions in the speech balloons on the bottom half of the "Deliverance" and "Forgiveness" pages. Give groups time to work. Then, beginning with the "Joshua" group, have groups report on what they wrote in their speech balloons.

The following are some suggested answers:

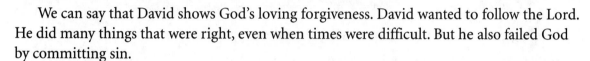

JOSHUA

What is the Bible character's name? (His name means "Jehovah is salvation.") *(Joshua.)*

What are five words that describe this person? *(Brave, obedient, willing, strong, humble.)*

What is the greatest thing about this person? *(He obeyed God even when almost everyone else didn't.)*

In Joshua 1:1–9, what are God's promises to Joshua? *(God would give Joshua every place he walked on. God would give him strength and victory. God would never leave him.)*

In Joshua 5:13—6:25, what did God do for Rahab? *(He saved or "delivered" her from death to live with the Israelites.)*

How does Joshua show us a picture of Jesus? *(Jesus delivered us from eternal death and He delivers us from our sins.)*

DAVID

What is the Bible character's name? (One of Jesus' names is "the Son of David.") *(David.)*

What are five words that describe this person? *(Brave, chosen, sinful, repentant, listened.)*

What is the greatest thing about this person? *(He admitted his sin and asked God to forgive him.)*

What happened in 2 Samuel 12:1–14 that shows David's character? *(When Nathan the prophet told David what he had done wrong, David was very sorry about his sin and asked the Lord to forgive him.)*

David wrote Psalm 32. What is his attitude toward sin? *(He thinks sin hurts people and makes them miserable. He says we should confess our sins right away. He is so glad that God forgives.)*

How does David show us a picture of what Jesus does for us? *(Jesus paid for our sins so that whenever we do something wrong, we can ask God and He will forgive us because of Jesus' blood.)*

When groups finish reporting, discuss the following questions:

- Which of these two Bible characters' lives taught you the most today? Why? *(Joshua, because I can see how obedience really pays off. David, because I didn't know before that God would forgive even the worst sins.)*

- Which of these two men do you think had the most difficult job? Why? *(Joshua, because he had to lead all those people across the river. David, because he was a king and when he failed, he was a bad example. I think he had to go a long way to get the people's confidence back.)*

- Which is hardest for you to do: asking God to help you avoid temptation or asking God to forgive you in a situation where you find it hard to swallow your pride? *(Allow students to respond.)*

- Joshua and David showed different kinds of courage. How would you describe Joshua's courage? *(When he was a spy, he stuck up for God's way when almost everyone else was against him. He asked the people to do the impossible—go across a river.)*

- How would you describe David's courage? *(He wasn't afraid to trust God and go against the giant, Goliath. It took courage to admit he was wrong and confess his sins.)*

APPLICATION: Real "Raisins" to Confess

Distribute handouts, scissors, and pencils. In our lesson today, we learned that the blessings of God depend on our obedience to Christ. We also found out that confessing our sins restores us to a right relationship with God and brings us joy. Proverbs 28:13 says, "He who conceals his sins does not prosper, but whoever confesses and renounces them finds mercy."

What sin or problem do you need deliverance from today? Think about that for a few moments. **Distribute the "Real 'Raisins' to Confess" handout. Work through the handout with the students.**

When you finish, say, Take a moment to pray as you confess your sin or problem to God right now. **Give students time to pray. Then say,** God has forgiven you of this sin. To show this, cut out the first raisin and throw it away. God no longer remembers it!

Give students time to cut out and throw away their raisins.

CHECK FOR UNDERSTANDING: Raisins in a Row

Hand out pieces of paper. Ask students to make a game card by drawing a large square and dividing it into sixteen smaller squares. Have them write one of the following names or places on each square in any order: Adam, Eve, Cain, Abel, Abraham, Isaac, Israelites, Moses, Egypt, Joshua, David, Rahab, Jericho, Jordan River, Red Sea, wilderness.

Give students raisins to use as markers. Read the following questions in random order, and have the students mark the correct answer by putting a raisin on that square. Continue until someone gets four in a row (horizontally, vertically, or diagonally). Applaud the winner. Play several times.

GAME QUESTIONS

1. Which leader caused water to turn to blood? *(Moses.)*
2. Who was the first man to sin? *(Adam.)*
3. What kind of land did the Israelites cross after they left Egypt? *(Wilderness.)*
4. Who was the first murderer? *(Cain.)*
5. Which boy almost became a sacrifice? *(Isaac.)*
6. Who was called the deliverer of the Hebrew people? *(Joshua.)*
7. What body of water did the people cross after they left Egypt? *(The Red Sea.)*
8. Who was willing to sacrifice his son? *(Abraham.)*
9. Who was tricked by the serpent? *(Eve.)*
10. What body of water did the people cross to enter the Promised Land? *(The Jordan River.)*
11. Who was Cain's brother? *(Abel.)*
12. What country was ruled by a Pharaoh? *(Egypt.)*
13. Who was a king of Israel? *(David.)*
14. Who was the woman saved by Joshua and his army in Jericho? *(Rahab.)*
15. What is the name of God's people? *(Israelites.)*
16. What city did Joshua conquer? *(Jericho.)*

MEMORY VERSE ACTIVITY: Raisin Relay

Joshua 1:9 / "Have I not commanded you? / Be strong and courageous. / Do not be terrified; do not be discouraged, / for the LORD your God will be with you wherever you go."

Before Class: Cut out fifteen raisin shapes from brown construction paper. (You could use the raisin on the "'Raisins' to Confess" page as a pattern.) Make three sets of "raisins," writing one portion of the verse on each raisin as shown. Use a heavy black marker. Tape one set of raisins on the board.

In our lesson today, we learned how Joshua and David trusted in God. Our memory verse gives us encouragement from God. Let's read it together. **Have the students read the verse together.** God is telling us that we do not need to be afraid because He is with us wherever we go.

Let's play a relay game to help us remember this verse. **Divide students into two teams. Give each team a set of raisins and give each person a straw. Have students mix up their raisins and place them (face up) about twenty feet away. Mark a starting line on the floor using masking tape, and have students line up.**

The object of this game is to get your verse back to your starting line in the correct order. When I say "go," the first person in each line will go and get the first part of the verse. Pick it up by sucking on the straw. With the verse part still connected to your straw, come back and put it down in front of your team. The next team member will go and get the next raisin. Do this until the verse is complete. When the verse is complete, read it together as a team.

Repeat this several times. Then have individuals say the verse to you if you choose.

WEEKLY ASSIGNMENT: Quick Confession

This week, have students review the names of all the Old Testament books.

The daily reading assignments are as follows:

Day 1—1 Samuel 1
Day 2—1 Samuel 3
Day 3—1 Samuel 8
Day 4—1 Samuel 9
Day 5—2 Samuel 2
Day 6—2 Samuel 5
Day 7—2 Samuel 7

Instruct your students to take home their "Real 'Raisins' to Confess" handouts and follow the directions on the sheet to confess any sin they may commit during the day. Encourage them to be prepared to tell the class what happened as a result of their confessing quickly.

Close in prayer, asking God to keep you and your students from giving in to temptation.

Deliverance

Joshua

This is a story about God's deliverance of His people.

Joshua was the leader who took over after Moses died. He was selected because he trusted God. This is how it happened. When the Hebrew people came to the land God promised to give them, God told them to send twelve spies into the land and scope it out. When they came back, ten of the spies said that the people who lived in the land were too strong and that the Hebrew people couldn't conquer them. Joshua and Caleb disagreed. They said that God is powerful and that with His help the people could conquer the land.

The people sided with the ten spies. God was angry with the people for not trusting in His promises. So He sent them back into the wilderness to wander around for forty years.

When the time was up and all the people who didn't believe in God's power had died, God told Joshua to lead the people across the Jordan River and into the Promised Land. Joshua led the people through the river, which parted just like the Red Sea had done years before.

God was with Joshua as his soldiers battled the people in the land. Whenever Joshua was in a tough situation, God delivered him from his enemies.

Joshua chapter 2   Joshua chapter 3   Joshua chapter 4

What is the Bible character's name? (His name means "Jehovah is salvation," the same phrase from which we get the name "Jesus.")

What are five words that describe this person?

What is the greatest thing about this person?

In Joshua 1:1–9, what are God's promises to Joshua?

In Joshua 5:13—6:25, what did God do for Rahab?

How does Joshua show us a picture of Jesus?

Forgiveness

David

This is a story of God's forgiveness of His people.

David was a man after God's own heart. When he was a boy, he trusted God to help him kill the giant, Goliath. Later, God sent Samuel the prophet to anoint David as king over Israel. David was a good king who served God with his whole heart.

David was also a sinner, just like we are. He did something that made God very displeased. One day when David was supposed to be out with his army fighting, he was relaxing in his house. He decided he would like to marry Bathsheba, a beautiful woman he saw next door to his palace. But there was a problem: she was already married.

David devised a terrible plan. He sent the woman's husband, Uriah, to the front lines of battle so that he would be killed by the enemy. That's exactly what happened. Then David married Bathsheba. He thought he was home free.

But Nathan the prophet came to David and said, "You have sinned." Then David realized that he had caused the murder of Uriah. He confessed his sin to God. God forgave David immediately of this terrible sin.

David's relationship with God was put back in order. He felt so good about that. But he still had to face the consequences of his actions. Some of his children rebelled against him. But David's relationship with God continued to grow.

2 Samuel chapter 5   2 Samuel chapter 9   2 Samuel chapter 24

What is the Bible character's name? (One of the names of Jesus is "the Son of David.")

What are five words that describe this person?

What is the greatest thing about this person?

What happened in 2 Samuel 12:1–14 that shows David's character?

David wrote Psalm 32. What is his attitude toward sin?

How does David show us a picture of what Jesus does for us?

Joshua and David

Joshua leading the people across the Jordan River

King David repenting of his sin in front of Nathan the prophet

Real "Raisins" to Confess

1 On the first raisin, write the sin or problem you need deliverance from today.

2 Read Joshua 24:3–13 and circle all the I's (which stand for God).

1. Problem or sin:

"I took your father Abraham from the land beyond the River and led him throughout Canaan and gave him many descendants. I gave him Isaac, and to Isaac I gave Jacob and Esau . . . Jacob and his sons went down to Egypt. Then I sent Moses and Aaron, and I afflicted the Egyptians by what I did there, and I brought you out. When I brought your fathers out of Egypt, you came to the sea, and the Egyptians pursued them with chariots and horsemen as far as the Red Sea. But they cried to the LORD for help, and he put darkness between you and the Egyptians; he brought the sea over them and covered them. You saw with your own eyes what I did to the Egyptians. Then you lived in the desert for a long time. I brought you to the land of the Amorites who lived east of the Jordan. They fought against you, but I gave them into your hands. I destroyed them from before you, and you took possession of their land . . .Then you crossed the Jordan and came to Jericho. The citizens of Jericho fought against you . . . but I gave them into your hands . . . So I gave you a land on which you did not toil and cities you did not build; and you live in them and eat from vineyards and olive groves that you did not plant."

2. What does this tell you about God?

On the second raisin, write what this tells you about God.

STEPS TO CONFESSING SIN:

1. As soon as you realize you sinned, admit to God what you did wrong.

2. Ask Him to forgive you.

3. Ask for His help to avoid that sin in the future.

4. If necessary, ask forgiveness from people you hurt when you sinned or repay anything you have taken or broken.

3 On the third raisin, write what you need God to accomplish for you concerning what you wrote on the first raisin.

3. God can accomplish this for me:

Elijah and Jeremiah

LESSON PLAN

OBJECTIVE: Students will learn how to serve God with power and courage.

APPLICATION: Students will commit themselves to ways of being heroes for God.

LESSON PLAN ELEMENT	ACTIVITY	TIME	SUPPLIES
Opening Activity	*I Stand Alone*	5–10	6 objects, 5 of which are the same color
Bible Story—1 Kings 18; Jeremiah 20, Elijah and Jeremiah	*Two Real Heroes*	7–10	Bible; "Hail to the Heroes!" handouts; pencils
Lesson Activity	*Heroes Hall of Fame*	10–15	1 copy of "Heroes Hall of Fame" master; card stock; glue; props for "Wax Museum" (see activity)
Application	*Be a Hero*	7–10	Bible; "Hail to the Heroes!" handouts; pencils
Check for Understanding	*Hail to the Hero*	3–5	All pictures from the time line; cellophane tape
Memory Verse Activity	*Elijah Stands Alone*	3–5	Dry-erase marker or chalk
Weekly Assignment	*Time to Be a Hero*	3–5	"Hail to the Heroes!" handouts

Prophets were men who were given a commission by God and usually had to stand alone to fulfill their position. Many were killed by their own people. Others spent years in exile or under the threat of death. In this lesson, your students will learn about two men who stood alone for God in the power of the Holy Spirit.

The most famous and dramatic of Israel's prophets, Elijah, was a complex man of the desert who confronted kings. His mission was to drive the worship of Baal out of Israel. Called "the grandest and most romantic character that Israel ever produced,"[1] Elijah exemplifies the power of a Spirit-led man.

He prophesied before King Ahab that there would be no rain or dew apart from his declaration. In Zarephath, he raised the widow's dead son to life (1 Kings 17:17–24). On Mount Carmel, he called down fire from heaven (1 Kings 18:16–40). And 2 Kings 2:7–11 records how Elijah struck the River Jordan with his cloak and the river divided so he and Elisha could cross on dry land. Then, as Elisha watched, Elijah was caught up into heaven in a chariot of fire.

Through Malachi, God promised to send another prophet like Elijah to Israel who would "turn the hearts of the fathers to their children, and the hearts of the children to their fathers" (Malachi 4:5,6). This prophecy was fulfilled in John the Baptist (Luke 1:17).

The Gospels of Matthew, Mark, and Luke record Elijah's appearance with Moses and Jesus on the Mount of Transfiguration. And one of the two witnesses mentioned in Revelation 11:4–6 is thought by many Bible students to be Elijah because of his power "to shut up the sky so that it will not rain during the time they are prophesying."

There is no doubt that Elijah was a Spirit-led man. But the real power of the prophet was not that he could perform miracles. The key to his abilities was his very personal relationship with God.

The same Holy Spirit who empowered the prophet indwells every child of God today. Jesus promised that we will have all the power we need when the Holy Spirit comes upon us (Acts 1:8). This power will enable us to be fruitful witnesses for Christ as we help fulfill the Great Commission.

Jeremiah was another prophet who stood alone. If you think it is difficult to stand for Christ in your home, in your school or workplace, or in your community, draw some encouragement from Jeremiah.

He was a prophet who endured. He acted as God's faithful messenger despite many attempts on his life. His enemies challenged his prophetic honesty. He lived in constant friction with religious and political authorities. And little wonder. He recommended national surrender to the Babylonian Empire and called Nebuchadnezzar, Judah's most hated enemy, the "servant of the Lord" (Jeremiah 25:9; 27:6). Furthermore, he was accused and convicted of treason.

Sometimes he complained to God about the misery of his office. But he was so sorrowful about the fallen condition of Israel that despite all of his hardships, he persisted in speaking the word of the Lord faithfully and earned the title of "weeping prophet." For twenty-three years Jeremiah spoke to the people repeatedly but they did not listen (Jeremiah 25:3). Could we have done that?

Jeremiah is an example to us of sticking to a task despite all odds—especially in a time when many Christians lack long-term commitment to the things of God. Like Jeremiah, we must be willing to be a witness who stands alone in the midst of incredible opposition to proclaim the Word of God and faithfully obey His commands.

Standing alone for God is a problem for elementary-age students who desperately want to be a part of the crowd. Yet we must equip them with the ability to stay faithful to what God has called them to do. Your students will remember lessons that are given through the stories of real people who stood alone.

---

1 Nelson Price, cited in the *Holman Bible Dictionary*, Trent C. Butler, general editor (Nashville: Holman Bible Publishers, 1991), p. 411.

LESSON PLAN

OPENING ACTIVITY: I Stand Alone

 Before Class: Find 6 objects that are all the same color except for 1. It could be 5 green leaves and 1 yellow, or 5 red apples and 1 green, or 5 blue balls and 1 red.

Ask volunteers to tell what happened after they confessed their sins as described on the "'Raisins' to Confess" handout.

Set the objects on a table in front of the class. Take a look at these objects.

- How are they all alike? *(They are all leaves, or whatever you have selected.)*

- How are they different? *(One is a different color.)*

That one stands out. We all notice it.

- Have you ever been in a situation where you stood alone? *(Allow students to share. Mention possible scenarios like being the only boy or girl at a party, or wearing casual clothes when everyone else is dressed up.)*

Sometimes we have to stand up for things we believe in. Other times we are the only ones who believe that way and we have to stand alone. Let's do an activity to help us understand how this might feel. **Have students form a circle. Choose a volunteer to be in the middle. Have everyone perform an action together while the volunteer does something different. The individual's action should be something that is outrageous or that would cause the others to stare. Some ideas are given below:**

CIRCLE CROWD	VOLUNTEER IN MIDDLE
Sing *God Bless America*.	Act and gobble like a turkey.
Tap a foot rhythmically on the floor.	Dance like Big Bird (flap wings and sing).
March around in a circle.	With arms outstretched, buzz around like an airplane.
Snap their fingers.	Hop like a frog and say, "Ribbit."
Clasp arms and sway back and forth.	Crow like a rooster.

After each activity, ask the volunteer in the middle how he or she felt during the action. Next, have everyone do the silly action together and ask how the volunteer felt then. He or she should acknowledge that the action was easier to do when everyone did it.

When finished say: Our Bible story today is about two men who stood alone for God. Let's hear about how they stood alone.

BIBLE STORY: Two Real Heroes

In our activity, the person who stood alone did some crazy things. But our story today is about two men who stood alone to do what God wanted them to do. We could call them real heroes.

- What do you think makes a person a hero? *(Being very strong and brave. Doing something that no one else can do. Not being afraid.)*

Distribute the "Hail to the Heroes!" handouts and pencils. On your handout, you will see an outline of a hero. I'm going to give you two examples of heroes in the Bible. As I tell their stories, write down the qualities that make each one a hero. When we finish with the story, we'll discuss what you wrote down.

As you relate the following events, point to the appropriate pictures on your time line. So far in the Old Testament, we learned about creation and about Adam and Eve, the first two people on earth. Then we heard about the forming of a nation, called Israel, when Moses led the Israelite people out of Egypt and to the Promised Land. Next, we learned about Joshua, who helped build the nation in the Promised Land, a time when judges ruled the nation. Then we learned about the times of the Israelite kings, especially about David who was the best known of the kings.

We've covered a lot of history. Things look pretty good for the nation whose people are called God's people. But now we'll turn to a dark time in that nation's history. After the reigns of two godly kings, King David and his son, King Solomon, the nation was ruled by wicked kings and turned away from God. The people didn't get along with each other, and finally the nation split into two parts. God was displeased with His people. He kept warning them to turn back to Him or suffer the consequences. One of the ways God warned His people was by speaking through prophets. The prophets were able to accomplish God's will and be His messengers by being filled with the Holy Spirit.

The prophets were given an assignment by God which they were to follow, whether or not it meant harm to themselves. The prophets warned the people. Many times, the people didn't like the message that the prophet was bringing, so they made fun of the prophet, hurt him in some way, and sometimes even killed him.

When God sent the prophet Elijah to the people in Israel, Ahab was the king. He was very wicked. The Bible says of Ahab, "He set up an altar for Baal [an idol] in the temple of Baal that he built in Samaria. Ahab also made an Asherah pole [a wicked type of worship] and did more to provoke the LORD, the God of Israel, to anger than did all the kings of Israel before him" (1 Kings 16:32,33). Because Ahab was so wicked, he hated Elijah.

Elijah told Ahab that it wouldn't rain for years and that all the crops would die. During this time of drought, God fed Elijah and took care of him. But Ahab was trying to find Elijah to kill him. Then God told Elijah to go speak to Ahab.

This is how Elijah answered God's call: "As the LORD Almighty lives, whom I serve, I will surely present myself to Ahab today" (1 Kings 18:15).

Point out the picture of Elijah from the "Elijah and Jeremiah" page. When Elijah and Ahab met on the top of Mount Carmel, the people gathered around to see what would happen. Ahab accused Elijah of being the "troubler of Israel" because he thought Elijah was responsible for the drought.

Elijah talked to the people who were gathered there. "How long will you waver between two opinions? If the LORD is God, follow him; but if Baal is God, follow him" (1 Kings 18:21). Elijah was challenging the people to follow God and to turn away from Baal worship. But the people didn't say anything.

Then Elijah proposed a test to show the people who the real God was. It was a brave thing to say. **Read 1 Kings 18:22–24.**

Elijah let the prophets of Baal go first. They built an altar to their god and put wood and a bull on the altar as a sacrifice. Then they called on Baal's name from morning until noon, asking him to burn up the sacrifice. "O, Baal, answer us!" they shouted (1 Kings 18:26). But guess what? Baal did not answer. The prophets danced around the altar to try to get his attention, but nothing happened.

At noon, Elijah began to tease them, "Shout louder! Isn't he a god? Maybe he's busy or traveling or asleep!"

The prophets of Baal shouted louder and began to cut themselves to make their god do something. But nothing happened.

When evening came, it was Elijah's turn. He repaired the altar to the LORD. (The people had let it go to ruin.) Then he put wood on it and the bull for the sacrifice. He dug a ditch around the altar and had some men fill it with water. Three times, the men poured water over the bull and the wood until the ditch overflowed with water.

Then, this is what happened. **Read 1 Kings 18:36–39.**

Isn't that amazing? The people began to call upon God when they saw the miracle God did. Why was Elijah the only one who stood up for God at first? Elijah was very brave to face the king who wanted to kill him, the prophets of Baal who wanted to make him look bad, and the people who didn't stand behind him. Elijah was able to stand alone because he relied on the power of the Holy Spirit.

Right after this miracle, God told Elijah that rain would begin again. Elijah told Ahab, and sure enough, the sky began to fill with clouds and the rains came.

Jeremiah was a prophet of God who also stood alone in the power of the Holy Spirit.

While Jeremiah was a prophet, Israel was once again unfaithful to God. They did all kinds of evil and worshiped idols. God sent Jeremiah to tell them that God was going to punish them. It was not a pleasant message to bring. Jeremiah knew that his message would make many people angry at him.

One day God sent Jeremiah to a potter's house. (A potter makes pots out of clay.) The potter was shaping something from clay, but the clay was marred. The pot was ruined. So the potter took the clay and made a different kind of pot.

God said to Jeremiah, "This is like what I will do to Israel. I am like the potter. I made Israel. I can do anything I want to do with what I made. Anytime I decide I want to destroy what I made, I can do that. If I want to take my nation out of the land, I can do that. But if My people repent of their bad behavior, I will not allow the disaster I have planned to happen to the nation."

Would you like to give that message to people? It is a hard message. And when the leaders heard the message, they got very angry. Jeremiah even told Pashhur, the chief officer, that he was wicked and needed to change his ways (Jeremiah 20:1–6). The chief officer of the temple had Jeremiah beaten and throw in prison. He was put into stocks, which are wooden pieces put around the wrists and ankles of a prisoner. But Jeremiah did not change his message. He stayed faithful to God and what God had told him to do.

Jeremiah kept right on warning the people. Like all prophets of God, he told what would happen in the future. Years later, the priests and other false prophets got so mad at him that they wanted to kill him. Jeremiah still did not change his message. At that time, the people and the officials stood up for Jeremiah and said that Jeremiah was speaking God's words.

Years after that, government officials got so mad at Jeremiah that they threw him into a cistern, which is a kind of well. There was no water in the cistern, but Jeremiah sank down into mud and couldn't get out. Then one brave man came to Jeremiah's rescue. **Point out the picture of Jeremiah in the cistern from the "Elijah and Jeremiah" page.**

Jeremiah suffered many things for the sake of God. Prison, threats of death, danger, ridicule, lack of food, and sorrow. But he stayed true to God.

- What did you put down as qualities of a hero? (*Allow students to give their thoughts. Add qualities such as bravery, courage, faithfulness, staying true to God, standing alone, doing what is right no matter what.*)

- Think of someone you know who you would describe as a hero. Why is that person a hero? (*Allow students to name people and give qualities.*)

- Do you think a hero is ever afraid? Why or why not? (*Yes, because everyone is afraid when bad things happen to them. No, because a hero never gets afraid.*)

Heroes get angry. Heroes feel afraid. Heroes feel lonely. These feelings don't go away just because they have to do something hard. I'm sure Jeremiah felt lonely in jail. I'm sure Elijah was afraid when he had to meet the king who wanted to kill him. But they did what God asked them to do in spite of their feelings. That's what a hero does.

- How can you do something difficult even though your feelings get in the way? (*Just get tough. Try to not think about my feelings.*)

These two were real heroes because they did difficult things in the power of God's Holy Spirit. They didn't try to do it in their own strength. Even though both Elijah and Jeremiah stood alone when no one came to stand beside them, they weren't really alone because they had God's Spirit inside them, helping them, giving them the right words to say, and making them brave and strong. That's what a real hero is. He or she is a person who does what is right with the help of God.

LESSON ACTIVITY: Heroes Hall of Fame

 Before Class: Cut apart the biographies on the "Heroes Hall of Fame" and glue them onto card stock.

Also, gather props for students to use in the "wax museum" activity.

Teaching Tip: To add to the fun, you may consider having another class come in to see your "Heroes Hall of Fame" or take your group to other classrooms after you finish the lesson.

Divide the class into five groups.

How many of you have ever been to a wax museum? It is a place that displays wax statues of well-known people. Some wax museums have statues of Hollywood stars or famous musicians. Today, we are going to make our own wax museum of heroes. They will come from the Bible stories we have studied. Your group will be assigned one of these heroes, and you will use the materials provided to make a "wax figure" out of one of your group members. You can also add other props to make your character seem more lifelike. One person in your group will be the museum guide for your hero and will read the card provided when everyone is finished.

Assign one of the five characters to each group and give each group the appropriate card. Set out the materials and give students 5 to 7 minutes to assemble their character and practice the "tour dialogue" from the card. You can help groups be more creative by suggesting that Moses' group make a stone tablet of commandments or a staff, Elijah's group make an altar, and so forth.

When groups finish, have them present their heroes. The characters should remain still like a figure in a wax museum while the card is read.

APPLICATION: Be a Hero

So now we've seen how Bible heroes followed God and stood alone in their faith. But what about you? Are you a Bible hero? God is calling you to be a hero for Him, to stand alone, and to tell others about Jesus.

Jeremiah shows us an example of the kind of call God gives people to work for Him. This is what Jeremiah wrote:

Read Jeremiah 1:4,5. When Jeremiah heard the call, he was afraid. He said: **Read verse 6.**

Jeremiah was saying that he didn't feel able to do what God asked of him. That he was too weak. This is how God answered: **Read verses 7–10.**

God was telling Jeremiah that he didn't have to worry about being strong enough because God would make him strong. God would give him the words.

That's what God wants to do for you. Are you ready? Is that what you want to do? Can you stand alone for God when your friends do what's wrong? Can you tell someone about Jesus even when that person makes fun of you for being "religious"? Will you help others who are hurting even if it costs you time and perhaps even some money? Will you be God's Elijah or Jeremiah today?

Take out your "Hail to the Heroes!" handout and your pencils, and I'll give you a few minutes to fill out the bottom half of the page. Think about what a hero for God would and would not do. Write down your thoughts.

Give students a few minutes to write. Then discuss what they wrote in each column. Some answers are listed below.

THINGS A REAL HERO WOULD DO	THINGS A REAL HERO WOULD NOT DO
Pray about a problem	Forget to pray
Follow the rules in the Bible	Disobey God's rules
Tell people about God's love	Go along with the crowd to do what's wrong
Be kind to people who are mean	
Do what's right even when everyone else is doing what's wrong	Keep quiet when someone says something bad about God
Listen to people who are sad	Avoid doing what's right because of fear
Know what's right (by studying the Bible) so he or she can do what's right	Disregard good rules because they are hard to keep
Ask God to fill him or her with the Holy Spirit	Be proud and refuse to change when he or she needs to
	Not listen to God's Word

When you finish your discussion, say, I'm going to give you a few minutes to pray and talk to God about being His hero. Ask God to help you be His hero, no matter what happens to you. Tell Him that you want to obey Him and that you want His Holy Spirit to fill you with His power to do the right thing. After you pray, if you sincerely made this decision to be God's hero, sign your name at the bottom of your page. This decision is for your eyes only. It is between you and God.

Give students time to pray and sign. Then close with a prayer of thanksgiving to God for allowing us to be His heroes and for giving us the power to do what's right. Have the students put their handouts in a place where they can be kept confidential. Perhaps students can turn over their papers on a table. Then go on to the next activity.

CHECK FOR UNDERSTANDING: Hail to the Hero

 Before Class: Remove all the pictures from your time line and mix them up.

Gather students in a semi-circle around the time line. Have volunteers come up and select one of the pictures and tell who the person is and why he or she is a hero. For the creation picture, have the volunteer tell how God helps us be heroes. For the Adam and Eve picture, emphasize how they followed God after they disobeyed Him. Then have each volunteer tape the picture in the appropriate place on the time line.

MEMORY VERSE ACTIVITY: Elijah Stands Alone

1 Kings 18:21a—"Elijah went before the people and said, 'How long will you waver between two opinions? If the LORD is God, follow him.'"

Write the verse on the board.

In our story today, we learned that Elijah and Jeremiah stood alone for God. Our memory verse speaks of that very thing. Let's read it together. **Read the verse together.** The second part of the verse says that the people said nothing. They don't speak up for God. So we will not learn that part of the verse. To learn our verse today we are going to play a game called "Elijah Stands Alone."

Have the students form a circle. I am going to choose some of you to stand inside the circle. You will be Elijah and the people. **Select three or four volunteers. You can appoint one of them to be Elijah or allow the volunteers to decide who it will be. It must be kept secret from the rest of the group.** I will say the reference, "1 Kings 18:21a," and then the people who are forming the circle will say together, "Elijah went before the people and said." Then one person will guess which of the volunteers in the middle is Elijah. If the guess is incorrect, the volunteer in the middle says nothing. That is just like the people in Elijah's time—they said nothing. Then I will repeat "1 Kings 18:21a." The circle will once again say, "Elijah went before the people and said." Then another person on the outside circle will choose someone else in the middle. If the person chosen is Elijah, he or she will say the second part of the verse, "How long will you waver between two opinions? If the Lord is God, follow him." Then the two people will exchange places. The volunteers in the middle will choose a new Elijah, and the game will start again.

Continue until you feel the verse has been memorized. Allow students to say the verse to you individually if you choose.

 Teaching Tip: Allow students to read from the board at the beginning of the game, but erase the verse as the game proceeds.

WEEKLY ASSIGNMENT: Time to Be a Hero

To help students memorize the books of the Bible, have them review the names of all the Old Testament books.

For their Bible Reading Journals, have students select a chapter from each of the five sections of the Old Testament to read on each of the days.

Now it is time to begin your hero adventure. Take your "Hail to the Heroes!" handout home and put it where you can see it. Perhaps you can hang it in your bedroom. Even heroes fail sometimes, so don't get discouraged if you fail to stand alone for God. If you do, tell God you're sorry, then ask for His help and to be filled with His Holy Spirit. Keep working at being a hero for God. You will succeed!

Close in prayer, asking God to help those students who have committed themselves to being a hero for God.

Hail to the Heroes!

Wanted: A Real Hero

Things a real hero would do	Things a real hero would not do

Signature _____

Elijah and Jeremiah

Elijah and the prophets of Baal

Jeremiah in the cistern

Heroes Hall of Fame

Moses

This hero was born as a slave in Egypt but was adopted by a princess. He was raised in a palace. One day he lost his temper and killed an Egyptian. He fled into the desert for his life. He spent 40 years in the desert tending sheep. When Moses was 80 years old, God spoke to him through a burning bush. God asked him to stand up for God and to demand that the Pharaoh let the Israelite slaves leave Egypt. This hero took up the task and led over a million people out of Egypt to the Promised Land.

Joshua

This hero was born in Egypt. He and his people left Egypt to follow Moses to the land God had promised them. When they finally reached that great land, he and 11 other men were sent to scout out the new land and report back to Moses. They found that the land was filled with good things to eat and was a wonderful place to settle. But it was also filled with strong, fierce people. Ten of the men said it would be impossible to go in and take the land. Only Joshua and a man named Caleb stood alone. They said that God was on their side and that they could conquer the land. But the people listened to the other ten men. God was very unhappy with Joshua's people. But He was very pleased with Joshua and Caleb. They showed great faith. Joshua went on to become a great leader of the people of Israel.

Elijah

This hero lived in Israel when everyone was worshiping an idol named Baal. Almost all of Elijah's people had forgotten God. The king even issued a decree that anyone worshiping God would be put to death. God told Elijah to take the king a message from God. Elijah stood alone and confronted the king with the message that God would punish the king for his wickedness. Then, before the entire nation, Elijah challenged the enemies of God to a contest. They were to call on their god to send fire down from heaven to burn up the sacrifice. Then Elijah would call on the true God. The prophets of Baal prayed the whole day and nothing happened. Then Elijah poured water over his altar and called on God. Fire came down from heaven and—even though it was all soaking wet—the altar and everything on it burned up. Elijah then testified that this was the work of the true God. This hero was not afraid to stand up for God.

David

This hero was born in Israel. He grew up tending his father's sheep. He first showed his bravery as a young boy by killing the giant Goliath who was threatening the army of God. One day his father sent him to bring food to his brothers who were serving in the army. When he got to the army camp, he saw that everyone was afraid of the enemies, the Philistines. Each day, a huge Philistine soldier came out and asked for an Israelite soldier to fight him. If the Israelite won, the Philistines would surrender. But if the Israelite lost, they would have to surrender. No Israelite was brave enough to fight the giant. Then David volunteered to fight because he knew God was on his side. He took several small stones and his slingshot. He didn't wear any armor. David came up to Goliath, let his slingshot fly, and hit Goliath in the forehead. Goliath was killed and the Philistine army ran away. One day the prophet Samuel came and anointed David as the next king of Israel. David obeyed God and was a great king. He obeyed God even when it seemed like his enemies were stronger than he was. God always gave him the victory. The Bible records that David was a man after God's own heart.

Jeremiah

Jeremiah was a man who answered God's call even when he didn't feel able to do the job. But when God said He would give him strength and the words to say, Jeremiah obeyed God. To show Jeremiah the message he was to bring, God sent Jeremiah to a potter's house. The potter was making a clay pot, but the clay was not good. So the potter scrapped that pot and started to make another. God told Jeremiah to tell the Israelites that He had created their nation, and He could do whatever He wanted with them. If they didn't obey, they would be sent out of their land and punished. If they turned their hearts to God, He would forgive them and make their land safe. Jeremiah took this warning of future punishment to the people of Israel because of the wicked way they were behaving. The officials and rulers in the temple got mad at Jeremiah. They didn't want to turn back to God because they liked worshiping idols. They arrested Jeremiah and put him in stocks. They threw him into a cistern full of mud where he would have starved to death. They wanted to have him killed. But Jeremiah stayed true to God. He told the people all the hard words God had given him to say. God protected Jeremiah from his enemies when he stood alone for God.

UNIT THREE

What's in the New Testament?

BOOK OBJECTIVE	To provide a survey of the Bible.
UNIT OBJECTIVE	To introduce students to the New Testament and how it tells the story of Jesus Christ and the beginning of the worldwide church.
LESSON 9: The Story of Jesus	*Objective:* To help students see the importance of Christ's life, death, and resurrection. *Application:* To teach students how to apply the Great Commandment and the Great Commission.
LESSON 10: The Story of the Church	*Objective:* To help students view the dynamic establishment of the first-century church. *Application:* To encourage students to examine their own talents and abilities to see how they can contribute to the work of the church.
LESSON 11: The Church Grows	*Objective:* To help students see how the gospel is amplified and defined through the New Testament writers. *Application:* To help students write a letter to someone asking for help in growing in Christ.
LESSON 12: The End of the Story	*Objective:* To help students learn about future events as given in the Book of Revelation. *Application:* To help students prepare for the coming of Christ.
LESSON 13: Jesus and the Tabernacle	*Objective:* To encourage students to reaffirm how God's plan, as revealed throughout the Bible, has always been to send His Son to die for our sins. *Application:* To help students praise God for His Word and how it shows us His Son and brings us closer to Him.

For more than fifty years, the most important book of my life—more meaningful than all the thousands of volumes in my personal library combined—has been the New Testament. I could not have survived spiritually without daily meditating upon the truths contained in this remarkable and supernatural book.

The New Testament is not just the words of mere men, but of God as the Holy Spirit inspired men of old to record these holy, life-changing truths. As I meditate on them day after day and night after night, my life is more and more conformed to the image of Christ through the power of the Holy Spirit.

No truths ever penned by man have such revolutionary potential, such explosive power to transform lives as the truths recorded in this God-inspired New Testament.

As a happy pagan in my secular years, I sometimes read the New Testament without comprehension and wondered how anyone could ever enjoy or even make sense out of it (1 Corinthians 2:11–14). Then I became a believer and experienced what Jesus describes in John 3 as the new birth. I became a new creation in Christ (2 Corinthians 5:17). The same Holy Spirit who transformed my life and helped me fall in love with our Lord Jesus Christ began to minister to me through His holy, inspired Word. Thus it soon became the most important source of spiritual nourishment of my life.

Through the years, I have read hundreds of books, numerous biographies, and all kinds of theological treatises, but all of them together have not even begun to make the kind of contribution to my spiritual growth as the truths contained in the New Testament. I read it, study it, memorize it, and meditate on it. Daily I am refreshed by it.

The New Testament reveals the mystery of God's marvelous plan to liberate us from the darkness and gloom of Satan's kingdom and bring us into the kingdom of His dear Son (Colossians 1:13,14). Billions of people around the world have not yet heard of this plan. Many within your own community—your friends, neighbors, loved ones—have yet to respond to God's love and forgiveness by receiving Christ into their lives. I urge you to introduce all who will listen to the message of God's grace that you will find explained in these lessons.

This study will help you and your students understand God's plan of redemption as fully revealed in the New Testament. How wonderful it is for your preteens to be able to grasp the significance of this collection of Gospels and letters to the church at their young age! I urge you to study the lessons carefully, applying the truths you learn to your own life before you teach them to your students. Share your adventure in the New Testament with them so that they can catch the vision and excitement of knowing Christ.

The Story of Jesus

LESSON PLAN

OBJECTIVE: Students will see the importance of Christ's life, death, and resurrection.

APPLICATION: Students will apply the Great Commandment and the Great Commission to their lives.

LESSON PLAN ELEMENT	ACTIVITY	TIME	SUPPLIES
Opening Activity	*Four Views*	7–10	Bibles; 4 photos of the same subject from different viewpoints
Bible Story—Assorted Scriptures from the Gospels; the death and resurrection of Jesus	*Darkness and Light*	10–15	Bibles; small cardboard box; sharp knife; flashlight; 1 copy of "The Story of Jesus" master; scissors; children's evangelistic booklet (optional)
Check for Understanding	*The Center of History*	3–5	The Old Testament time line and all the pictures; "The Story of Jesus" pictures; tape
Lesson Activity	*Four Colors*	7–10	Bible; pieces of red, yellow, blue, and green cellophane or translucent plastic cups; 4 flashlights; rubber bands
Application	*The Two Greats*	7–10	Bibles; "Two Sides of a Coin" handouts; pencils; coin
Memory Verse Activity	*Pass the Light*	3–5	4 flashlights; dry-erase marker or chalk
Weekly Assignment	*Two Sides of a Coin*	3–5	"Two Sides of a Coin" handouts

The four Gospels are like four photographs of the same scene taken by four different photographers. Each photo is viewed from a unique angle and highlights distinct aspects of the action on the scene. When viewed together, the four photographs give a well-rounded view of what happened during the event.

Each of the Gospel writers, Matthew, Mark, Luke, and John, writes about the life of Jesus from a different perspective. Matthew presents Jesus as the Kings of kings. Matthew writes to the Jews to prove that Christ is their promised Messiah and the eternal King of kings and Lord of lords. Matthew also shows how Jesus fulfilled prophecy and how He is the Person who will usher in God's kingdom. This book is the link between the Old and New Testaments.

Mark shows Jesus as the humble servant who cared deeply for people. Although Matthew precedes Mark in the New Testament, Mark is considered the first of the four Gospels to be written. Mark addresses his book to the Roman Christians. Romans were a practical people and did not care about Jewish history and beliefs. The Romans loved action so Mark writes a brief Gospel full of Jesus' miracles and deeds, not His sermons.

The most comprehensive of the Gospels, Luke presents an accurate account of the life of Christ as the perfect Man and Savior. Luke delves into Christ's human nature. Luke writes his Gospel to the Greeks, a cultured people who, he knew, would be captivated by Jesus as the perfect Man, an idea prevalent in Greek mythology. Luke also portrays our Lord's concern for His followers and friends and shows His tenderheartedness toward the poor, despised, and sinful. Luke also shows how Christ lived in total dependence on the Holy Spirit.

John shows Jesus as the Son of God. Called the "Gospel of Love," John's book has won the affection of Christians who turn to it first for inspiration. Because of its universal appeal, this Gospel is usually the first to be translated into a foreign language or dialect, and it is the most widely distributed of the Gospels. John seeks to prove conclusively that Jesus is the Son of God and that all who believe in Him will have eternal life. John focuses on the uniqueness of Jesus, portraying Him as the Creator who became flesh and dwelt among men as the Lamb of God "who takes away the sin of the world" (John 1:29).

Each of these portrayals is accurate, but when put together, they give a wonderful picture of the eternal, complex, and perfect nature of our Lord, Jesus Christ. As we read them, we see a progression of teaching in each book. Matthew, for example, ends with the Resurrection; Mark closes with the Ascension; Luke gives the promise of the Holy Spirit; and in John, our Lord breathes the Holy Spirit upon His disciples and speaks of His return.

As you teach this lesson, you will continue to use the time line. The added pictures will help your students locate the New Testament events within the span of time.

LESSON PLAN

OPENING ACTIVITY: Four Views

Before Class: Find four photos of the same scene. It could be four snapshots of a tourist attraction such as the Grand Canyon, four portraits of the same person, or four views of the inside of a room.

Make sure each student has a Bible. Open your Bible to the New Testament.

The Old Testament predicted that a Messiah would come who would pay for the sins of the world. The Israelite nation eagerly awaited the coming of this Messiah.

Then Jesus, the Messiah, came. He was born in a stable, as we've all heard in that familiar Christmas story. He grew up to be a Perfect Man. He never sinned and He always obeyed God, His Father. He performed miracles, taught the people, and trained twelve disciples. The birth of Jesus is the beginning of the New Testament.

Whereas the Old Testament predicted the future coming of the Messiah, the New Testament tells what happened when He came and what happened after He returned to heaven. The first four books of the New Testament—Matthew, Mark, Luke, and John—all describe Jesus' life on earth and His death.

- Why do you think that four writers told the same story? (*I'm not sure. Because they all wanted to tell what they saw.*)

Hold up the first photo you brought.

- What is in this picture? (*Quickly have students tell what they see in the picture.*)

When we look at a picture, we see some things, but other things might be hidden from our view.

Hold up the second photo.

- This picture shows the same scene. What's different in this view? (*Allow students to describe what they see that's different.*)

When we see a second view of the same picture, we get more information about the scene.

Hold up the third photo.

- Do you see anything new in this picture? (*Allow students to respond.*)

Hold up the fourth picture.

- Do you see anything different in this picture? (*Allow students to respond.*)

- Which picture did you like best and why? (*Allow students to respond.*)

Isn't it interesting that different photos give us a different view of the same scene? That's similar to what happened when four writers wrote about Jesus' life and death. They each took a different view of what happened. They each wrote the absolute truth; but they each wrote about it from the perspective they saw and what God told them to write. Just like these four photos showed different parts of the same picture, the first four books in the New Testament give different views of the life of Jesus. They are called the Gospels. This is what each told about Jesus:

Point out each Gospel in your Bible as you talk about it. Have your students find each book in their Bibles. Matthew described Jesus as the King of kings and the Lord of lords. Matthew wanted the Jewish people to know that Jesus was the King they had been waiting for. In this way, Matthew was like a bridge between the Old Testament and the New Testament.

Mark described Jesus as a servant who helped people and cared deeply for them. Mark was writing to the Romans, people who liked action. Mark's Gospel shows lots of action about what Jesus did.

Luke showed how Jesus was a perfect Man and our Savior. He told about how Jesus cared about His followers, the poor, and the sinful. Luke was writing to the Greeks, people who had myths about superhumans who could overcome anything. Of course, Jesus is the only true "superhuman" because He is God and can do everything.

John's book is sometimes called the "Gospel of Love." John shows how much Jesus loves us. John also proves that Jesus is the Son of God and the Lamb of God "who takes away the sin of the world" (John 1:29). John's book is the most read Gospel and has been translated into many, many languages.

In our Bible Story, we'll hear more about this fantastic story—Jesus' life, death, and resurrection.

BIBLE STORY: Darkness and Light

Before Class: On one end of a small box, cut out a cross-shaped hole. Place a flashlight into the box. During the lesson, you will turn on the flashlight so that it shines a cross-shaped light onto the wall. Practice with the box and flashlight to make sure you know how to shine the light at the appropriate time and that your room can be darkened enough to show the light.

Cut apart the pictures on "The Story of Jesus" copy.

The most important event in all four books is the story of how Jesus was arrested, put on trial, sentenced to death, nailed to a Roman cross, died, and rose again on the third day. Let's tell this story.

Make sure your students have their Bibles open. As much as possible, have your students help you tell the story. If they aren't that familiar with the story, tell it yourself.

Help your students find each part of the story in each Gospel as you tell it. It's not necessary to read the verses, but just to show the students that all four Gospels relate the same story in different ways. As you tell the story, hold up the pictures of Jesus' death and resurrection from "The Story of Jesus."

1. Jesus is arrested. Matthew 26:47–56; Mark 14:43–51; Luke 22:47–53; John 18:1–11

2. Jesus is put on trial. Matthew 26:57–67; Mark 15:1–20; Luke 22:63—23:25; John 18:12–40

3. Jesus is crucified. Matthew 27:32–44; Mark 15:21–32; Luke 23:26–43; John 19:16–27

4. Jesus dies. Matthew 27:45–56; Mark 15:33–41; Luke 23:44–49; John 19:28–37

5. Jesus is buried. Matthew 27:57–61; Mark 15:42–47; Luke 23:50–56; John 19:38–42

6. Jesus arises from the dead. Matthew 28:1–15; Mark 16:1–14; Luke 24:1–12; John 20:1–18

Darken the lighting in the room. Then tell this part of the story.

The day that Jesus died was very sad. The only Person who had never sinned had been put on a cross and killed in a painful, horrible way. Some of the people who loved Jesus were standing near the cross watching. They were crying. They couldn't understand why their Lord had to die.

When Jesus took His last breath, the sky darkened like nighttime—even though it was noon. People got scared, wondering what was happening. The darkness was God's way of showing what a terrible thing it was that Jesus had to die.

But the darkness could not last. Something tremendous was happening. **Turn on the flashlight that you placed inside the box and shine the cross on the wall.**

Our whole world is in darkness right now. It is in the darkness of sin. No one can find his or her own way out of this darkness. There is nowhere to go to escape. But there is one light. That light is Jesus. The darker the world gets, the more the light of Jesus shines through. His cross is the light we need to find our way out of the darkness of sin.

Optional Activity: Instead of looking up the following verses and conducting the discussion, go through a children's evangelistic booklet such as *Would You Like to Belong to God's Family?* (See the Resources at the back of this book for ordering information.) Be sure to allow time to counsel students who indicate a desire to receive Christ as their Savior. Give each person who makes a decision a copy of the booklet to take home. At the back of the booklet are Christian growth principles that you can encourage the new believer to practice.

Read the following verses and ask the questions. As you discuss the answers, bring out the points in parentheses. The goal of this discussion is to lead unbelieving students to make a decision to trust Jesus as their Savior. Be sensitive to the Spirit's moving as you do so, and do not force any student to make a decision that he or she may not be ready to make.

Read Hebrews 9:27,28.

- Why did Jesus have to die? (*So He could pay for the sins we have committed. He sacrificed Himself so that we won't face judgment.*)

Read John 1:29.

- Why does the Bible call Jesus the Lamb of God? (*In the Old Testament, the priest killed a lamb on an altar to pay the penalty for the person's sin. The lamb was a picture of Jesus, who is the sacrifice for our sins. Jesus died in our place to pay the penalty for our sins.*)

Read Romans 6:23.

- Why is it so important to have your sins forgiven? (*If you don't have your sins forgiven, you will be eternally separated from God in a place of punishment called hell. There is no way you can make up for the wrongs you have done.*)

Read Romans 8:1,2.

- If we are sinners, and God cannot allow sin in heaven, how will we ever make it to heaven? (*We have to be sorry for our sins and agree to turn from them. We have to believe that Jesus died to pay for our sins, and we have to ask God to forgive us our sins because of what Jesus did.*)

Read Acts 16:31.

- If we pray in faith believing in Jesus, what will God do to answer our prayers? (*God will forgive our sins and adopt us into His eternal family. We will become a child of God and will one day live forever with Jesus.*)

Have you ever made this decision? Are you sure that you are a member of God's family? Perhaps right now you know that you are a sinner and that you have never asked God to forgive your sins. But you do believe that Jesus died for your sins and you want to become a child of God. If so, you can join God's family and have your sins forgiven by talking to God right now.

I am going to pray a prayer. In the prayer, I will talk to God about the decision you want to make right now. I will stop in the middle of the prayer to give you a chance to pray silently. When you do, simply say something like this: "Dear God, I know that I am a sinner. I have done many wrong things. I am sorry that I have disobeyed You and Your laws. I believe that Jesus died on the cross for my sins. Please forgive my sins and make me a member of Your family. Thank You. In Jesus' name, amen."

You do not have to say these words perfectly. Just say them from your heart.

For those of you who have already asked Jesus to be your Savior, also pray silently when I pause. Ask God to help any person in this room who is not a part of God's family to make that decision. Also thank God for forgiving your sins and thank Jesus for dying for you.

After I pause for a few moments to give you time to pray, I will close my prayer.

Pray a prayer similar to this one. Pause in the middle to give students time to talk to God silently. Then close your prayer.

Dear heavenly Father, I love You and know that You love me. I thank You so much for sending Your Son, Jesus, to the earth to die on a cross for my sins. I thank You that I am part of Your family. You know the heart of each person in this room. Speak to the heart of any person here who is not a part of Your family. I know that You want to forgive that person's sins and make him or her Your child. Thank You that You will do this for anyone who prays to You with a sincere heart. **Pause here to allow students to pray silently.**

Thank You, Lord, that You listened to each prayer that was prayed here today. Please help us obey You as Your children should. Help us grow to be more like Your Son, Jesus. In Jesus' name, amen.

Tell the students that if they made a decision to become part of God's family, they should come and tell you before the next activity begins. If you think a student may have made a decision and that student doesn't approach you, privately and gently ask if he or she asked God for forgiveness during your prayer. Be prepared to counsel students about their new life in Christ if a decision to follow Christ was made.

CHECK FOR UNDERSTANDING: The Center of History

Before Class: Assemble your time line with all the Old Testament pictures. Draw a large red cross after the Old Testament part of the time line and add more paper (approximately 4 feet) for creating the New Testament time line.

Have students sit near the time line. Remind them that the Bible is divided into two parts, the Old and New Testaments, and that the parts are divided by the birth of Jesus. The cross then becomes the central event in history.

As we studied in our last unit, many of the events in the Old Testament pointed to the death and resurrection of Jesus. Let's see if you can remember any of these facts.

Allow volunteers to come up, point to a picture, and explain how it relates to God's plan to send Jesus to earth. Not all the pictures will relate. Following are some examples.

Adam and Eve—Adam and Eve were the first sinners. God sent Jesus to save people from their sins.

Noah and the ark—God saved Noah from destruction in the worldwide flood, and He will save believers from eternal destruction.

Abraham and Isaac—Just as Abraham was willing to sacrifice Isaac, God was willing to sacrifice His Son, Jesus. Although God kept Abraham from sacrificing Isaac, God did sacrifice His only Son.

The Passover—The people put blood on their doorposts to save themselves from death. Jesus' blood that was shed on the cross saves us from eternal death.

Moses and the Law—We all are guilty of breaking God's Law. We need a Savior, Jesus, to pay for our sins.

Joshua—He delivered his people from the enemies in the land. Jesus delivers us from our enemies, Satan and the world.

David—He was a great king of Israel. Jesus is our eternal King.

Elijah—He fought against the false prophets of Baal and won. Jesus won the battle against every false god.

Jeremiah—He spoke the truth about the coming of the Messiah. Jesus is the Messiah.

When finished, have a student tape up "The Story of Jesus" pictures (of Jesus' death and resurrection) next to the cross.

LESSON ACTIVITY: Four Colors

 Before Class: Using rubber bands, attach a different color of cellophane over each of the flashlights. Or if you are using colored plastic cups, have the students hold them over the flashlights.

Select four students to hold the flashlights. Have them stand or sit facing a blank wall at the front of the room.

Let's see what beautiful patterns we can make on the wall with our colors. **Dim the light in the room. Allow the four students to shine their flashlights on the wall in random patterns any way they choose. Then choose four other students and instruct them to make different patterns on the wall with the flashlights. Keep rotating students until everyone has had a chance to use a flashlight.**

Isn't it interesting how many different shapes and patterns we made using just four flashlights? Actually, the combinations are almost limitless. We could go on shining the lights differently for a long time.

Now think of how God wanted to show His truth through His Son, Jesus. All the truth of God was contained in this one Person, Jesus Christ. Jesus is the Light. That is one reason why God chose to have four different writers tell the story of Jesus.

Let's look at two very important truths that Jesus taught His followers. They are the most important ideas in the Bible.

Turn the light back on. The first truth is called the Great Commandment. **Have a good reader read Matthew 22:34–40.**

- What does Jesus mean when He says that the whole Law and the prophets hang on those two commandments? *(That every part of God's law depends on our loving God and others. When we love God and others, we obey all God's laws.)*

- How did Jesus obey both parts of this Great Commandment? *(Jesus loved His Father with all His heart, and always obeyed Him. Jesus loved people so much that He died for them.)*

Now let's look at the second truth that Jesus taught. It is called the Great Commission. **Have a good reader read Matthew 28:18–20.**

- What example did Jesus give us of how to obey the Great Commission? *(Jesus was always telling people about God. Jesus traveled around talking about how people could know God.)*

The Great Commission was the last command Jesus gave His followers before He went back to heaven. It was very important to Him. And the Great Commandment and the Great Commission are related to each other. If we love God and others, we will want to tell them about Jesus and how He has made the way for us to go to heaven.

When we obey the Great Commandment and the Great Commission, we become like those different colored lights. We shine for Jesus in every color of the rainbow. When people see how much we love them, they will listen to our words about how God loves them and wants them to be His children. We can tell people everywhere about God and His Son, Jesus.

APPLICATION: The Two Greats

Hold out a coin. Notice that this coin has two sides. This side is called "heads" and this side is called "tails." The coin couldn't exist without both sides.

That's the way it is with the two "Greats" in the Bible—the Great Commandment and the Great Commission. **Distribute the "Two Sides of a Coin" handout and make sure students have pencils and Bibles.**

This week, I want you to practice these two great commandments from Jesus. First, make sure you love the Lord your God with all your heart. Along with that, make sure you love the people around you like God loves them.

Then tell these people about Jesus. When you love them, your love will shine through and they will be more likely to listen when you talk about Jesus.

On the front of your coin on the top half, write a commitment to love God with all your heart. You could write, "God, I will love you the best." Or "God, help me to love you with all my heart."

Give students time to write. When they finish, say: Now, on the bottom half, write down at least two people you have a hard time loving. It could be a younger brother or sister, someone at school, or a neighbor. Keep this information private.

Give students time to write. When they finish, say: Turn your handout over and on the back of your coin, write the Great Commission. It is found in Matthew 28:19,20. **Give students time to write. When they finish, say:** Now write the name of at least one person that you would like to tell about Jesus. It can be a friend at school, a relative, or someone you see each week at the store or somewhere else.

> *Optional Activity:* If you used a children's evangelistic booklet in the Bible story, you may want to give each of your students the same booklet to help them tell others about Jesus. If you do, show them how to use the booklet by going through it with them.

MEMORY VERSE ACTIVITY: Pass the Light

"All authority in heaven and on earth has been given to me.

Therefore go and make disciples of all nations,

baptizing them in the name of the Father and of the Son and of the Holy Spirit,

and teaching them to obey everything I have commanded you.

And surely I am with you always, to the very end of the age."

Matthew 28:18–20

Write the memory verse on the board as shown above. Divide students into groups of six and have them stand in a line facing the board. Give the person in the front of each line a flashlight.

We learned that God's message is like a light to people living in the darkness. To show how we can bring the light of God's message to others who don't know Jesus as their Savior, let's use flashlights to help us memorize our verse. The first person in your line will turn on the flashlight. That shows that God gives us the message to tell others. This person will say the first line of the verse, turn off the flashlight, and pass it to the person next in line. That person will turn on the flashlight, say the second part of the verse, turn off the flashlight, and pass it on to the third person. Keep passing the flashlight until your line has said all parts of the verse. Some people may say more than one part of the verse by the time you are done.

Have the first person in each group begin. (All four groups will play at once.) Keep playing until the students learn the verse. Then erase the verse from the board and try again. Allow group members to help each other during this part of the game to avoid embarrassing students who have a harder time memorizing.

When finished, have individual students say the verse to you if desired.

WEEKLY ASSIGNMENT: Two Sides of a Coin

Today the students will begin to memorize the names of the New Testament books. In their journals, have them write the heading "Gospels" followed by the book names Matthew, Mark, Luke, and John, and the heading "History" followed by the book name Acts.

The daily Bible reading assignments are as follows:

Day 1—Matthew 1
Day 2—Matthew 2
Day 3—Mark 14
Day 4—Luke 22
Day 5—Luke 23
Day 6—John 20
Day 7—John 21

Make sure students have their "Two Sides of a Coin" handouts. Just as a coin is valuable when you go to buy something, practicing the Great Commandment and the Great Commission is a valuable thing to do for your spiritual life. God will bless you as you spend your life loving Him and loving others and telling people about Him.

Take your coin home and practice what you've written on it. See how God will bless you as you put into practice the truths that Jesus taught.

Close in prayer, asking God to help you and your students obey the Great Commandment and the Great Commission during the next week.

The Story of Jesus

The death of Jesus

The resurrection of Jesus

Two Sides of a Coin

Love the Lord your God with all your heart and with all your soul and with all your mind, and love your neighbor as yourself.

The Story of the Church

LESSON PLAN

OBJECTIVE: Students will view the dynamic establishment of the first-century church.

APPLICATION: Students will examine their own talents and abilities to see how they can contribute to the work of the church.

LESSON PLAN ELEMENT	ACTIVITY	TIME	SUPPLIES
Opening Activity	*Building Together*	7–10	Regular-size and mini-marshmallows; red, yellow, green, and blue food coloring; 1 Q-tip; toothpicks; construction paper scraps; glue
Bible Story—Acts 10; the Gentiles come into the Church	*Peter and Cornelius*	10–15	Bible; large white sheet; 1 copy of "Peter and Cornelius" master
Lesson Activity	*Using Our Talents and Abilities*	7–10	Bibles; guests to tell about what they do in church (see activity); dry-erase marker or chalk
Application	*Working Together*	7–10	Bibles; "What I Can Do" handouts; pencils; dry-erase marker or chalk
Memory Verse Activity	*Pass on the Message*	3–5	Bible
Check for Understanding	*Holy Spirit Help*	3–5	"Peter and Cornelius" picture; tape
Weekly Assignment	*Sent Out to Work*	3–5	"What I Can Do" handouts; pencils

A sequel to the Gospel of Luke, the Book of Acts portrays the birth and growth of the Christian Church. Acts is also a theological work that builds a strong case for the validity of Christ's claims and promises.

Luke's record of the coming of the Holy Spirit shows that the Church did not start or grow by its own initiative, but through the Holy Spirit who empowered the early Christians. He is the One who imparts the power in the lives of willing believers and guides them in their work for God.

The Book of Acts also describes the opposition and persecution that the Christians suffered at the hands of both Jews and Gentiles. This opposition, however, became a catalyst for the spread of Christianity. Rather than defeating the believers, persecution forced them to spread their message in increasing distances from the center, Jerusalem.

Acts is considered the connecting link between the life of Christ and the life of the Church and is a glimpse into the Christian world that gave birth to the Epistles. With a background in the early history of the Church, the teachings of Peter, Paul, and other New Testament writers become deeper and more meaningful.

In school, your students are beginning to grasp historical events. They will be studying national and statewide history. In turn, we can give them an introduction to the historical events that brought about the worldwide Church. Many of your students may have heard some of the stories in Acts, but they may not connect them to the exciting time when the message of Jesus Christ first began to be spread to people everywhere. This lesson will help students understand the transition from the lives of the disciples to the power of the first believers.

LESSON PLAN

OPENING ACTIVITY: Building Together

Before Class: Divide the regular-size marshmallows into four equal piles. Using a Q-tip, mark each group of marshmallows with a different color by dabbing food coloring on them. (Just a small spot will be enough.) Provide enough marshmallows so that each student gets at least four.

To protect the work surface, you may want to cover the table with paper.

Make four flags by cutting triangles out of construction paper and gluing them onto toothpicks.

Discuss with your students whether they were able to tell someone about Jesus in their commitment to help fulfill the Great Commission. Talk about how these people responded and what the students could do to help people understand more about Jesus as they keep on helping to fulfill the Great Commission. If your students used the booklet *Would You Like to Belong to God's Family?* to share their faith with others, make available more booklets so your students can continue using them.

When you finish your discussion, say: Does your school teacher talk a lot about cooperation in your classroom? Cooperation is important, but it's hard to do. Since we are all such different people with different personalities, sometimes it can be hard to get along well enough to cooperate on a project.

Today, we're going to talk about a different kind of cooperation. To help us understand the concept of cooperation, let's build a building.

Distribute at least four regular-size marshmallows to each student. The color doesn't matter, but make sure that each student has the same number of marshmallows. Set out the toothpicks, flags, and mini-marshmallows.

The rules for building your building are these:

1. As a group, you must decide on what kind of building to build. Will it be a castle? Or a skyscraper? You decide.

2. The next rule is that the regular-size marshmallows must be put on in a certain order. All the red ones must be on the bottom layer, the blue ones on the second layer, the green ones on the third layer, and the yellow ones on top. The mini-marshmallows can be used to help you build in any way you want. Use the toothpicks to hold your building together.

3. The last step in this building process is to put the flags on top. Assign four people to each put on one flag.

Okay, you can start.

Give students time to work. Notice how well they do at cooperating with each other. Also note which students end up with specific jobs, such as directing where the marshmallows will go, finding students with the right color marshmallows, adjusting the marshmallows to make them look better, putting on the flags, or any other specific task that develops during the building.

When students finish, compliment them on their job. Then ask:

- What was the most fun about building together? *(Seeing everything come together. Getting other people's ideas.)*

- Without saying anything critical about another person, what was the hardest part about working as a group? *(Some people didn't have the same ideas as I did. Knowing when to do something. There were so many people that it was hard to figure out what to do.)*

- How do you think this is like working together in a church? *(People have lots of different ideas, and they all have to put their ideas together. Sometimes you might not know what to do.)*

Just imagine that you are one of the disciples. You see Jesus go up in the clouds to be with His Father in heaven. Suddenly, you are faced with the job of building a church of believers who will one day cover the whole earth! (In the Bible, the word *church* can mean two things. It can mean all Christians all over the world, and it can mean a church building like ours where people meet to worship God.) How will you start? What will you tell people to do? Of course, building the new worldwide church was so much more complicated than the little job we did with the marshmallows. But this is the task that the new Christians faced when the church first began.

BIBLE STORY: Peter and Cornelius
Spread the white sheet on the floor and have students sit around the outside of the sheet, not touching the material.

When the church first began after Jesus went to heaven, only one kind of people were in the church. They were Jewish people. All the disciples were Jews. Jesus was a Jew. So the Jewish Christians got the idea that everyone had to become a part of the Jewish faith in order to be part of the church.

To show how this was, let's have two people sit on the sheet. **Select two people to sit on the sheet.** Only these two people can be part of the church. All the rest of you are not allowed in.

But of course, Jesus had given His disciples the Great Commission. In this command, Jesus told His followers to go to all the world to tell people about God's love. Something was wrong. How could the whole world hear if only Jewish people were allowed in the church?

God started to teach the first Christians about how much He loves every person on earth. He did this through Peter.

GROWING IN GOD'S WORD

Open your Bible to Acts 10. In a town called Caesarea lived a man named Cornelius. He was a centurion in the Roman army, which meant he was a high officer. He and his whole family loved God. One day he had a vision. An angel came to him and said, "God has seen your good works, and he wants you to talk to a man called Peter. Send some of your servants to bring Peter to your house."

So Cornelius immediately did what the angel told him to do.

Meanwhile, Peter went up on the roof of a house to pray while he was waiting for lunch. As the food was being prepared, he fell into a trance. He too saw a vision. A large sheet was being lowered from heaven by its four corners. **Point out the sheet on the "Peter and Cornelius" picture.** On the sheet he saw all kinds of creatures: reptiles, birds, and four-footed animals. A voice told him, "Get up, Peter, and eat these creatures."

Peter was horrified. Many of the animals on the sheet were ones that the Jewish faith forbid people to eat. This would be against Peter's faith. Peter exclaimed, "I've never eaten these unclean animals before!"

Then the voice said, "Don't call anything impure that God calls pure."

This happened three times, then the sheet was taken up to heaven and Peter woke up. Peter was confused about what the dream meant. Just then, two men came to the house. These were the two servants Cornelius had sent. The Holy Spirit said to Peter, "Go with these men. God has sent them to you."

The next day, Peter went with the two servants to Cornelius's house. Cornelius was expecting him and he had gathered friends and relatives to hear what Peter had to say. **Point out the crowd on the "Peter and Cornelius" picture.** When Peter came into the house, Cornelius knelt at Peter's feet. Peter said, "Get up. Don't worship me. I'm only a man."

Then Peter spoke to the large gathering of people. Peter said, "You know that Jews think they shouldn't have anything to do with Gentiles [people who aren't Jews]. But God has shown me that I should not call any person unclean or impure. Everyone is special to God." That, of course, was what God was trying to teach Peter through the vision of the sheet with all the animals.

Cornelius told Peter about the vision he had. Then Peter said, "I now realize how true it is that God does not show favoritism but accepts men from every nation who fear Him and do what is right. This is the message God sent to the people of Israel, telling the good news of peace through Jesus Christ, who is Lord of all." Then Peter explained all about Jesus' death and resurrection and how he had witnessed all that had happened to Jesus.

The people who were listening all trusted in Jesus and became Christians. They were now added to the church. Then Peter ordered that they all be baptized in the river. So they all were.

This is how God taught the people that anyone on earth can become part of the church by trusting in Jesus. God does not discriminate between people. He just looks at the heart.

One at a time, have each person who is sitting outside the sheet stand and have the students name a kind of person who is included in the church. This could be people of different races, from different countries, men, women, children, the old, the young, middle-aged. Then have that student move onto the sheet until all your students are seated on the sheet. Talk about how wonderful it is that God invited everyone to come into His church, not just the Jewish people.

- What is the only requirement for a person to become a member of God's family and a member of His worldwide church? *(To trust in Jesus Christ as your Savior.)*

- How does it make you feel to know that every person on earth is invited to be a part of God's church? *(I'm so glad that God loves everyone. I'm not surprised that God wants everyone to become a Christian because Jesus died for everyone.)*

Read Matthew 28:18–20, the Great Commission.

- How does the fact that God doesn't discriminate fit in with the Great Commission? *(God commanded us to go to all nations, so that fits with the fact that God wants every person to love Him and go to heaven.)*

- How do you think God feels about Christians who just want to have a certain type of person in their church? *(He feels sad. He wants them to change their opinion to include everyone.)*

I am so glad that God included everyone in the world in His plan to save people through the death of Jesus. If God did discriminate, there would be a good chance that I wouldn't have the chance to go to heaven. But God included me and He included you! Because of this, we need to give out the message of God's love and forgiveness to everyone we see, no matter whether people are rich or poor, educated or not educated, Jewish or Gentile, young or old.

Because God is so interested in telling everyone about His love, He had different ways of reaching them. In our Lesson Activity, we will see how different two of God's best preachers were—Peter and Paul.

LESSON ACTIVITY: Using Our Talents and Abilities

Before Class: Invite several people to come to class and tell your students about what they do in the church. Select people with various jobs, such as musician, pastor, teacher, usher, janitor. Instruct these people to explain to the students how their talents and abilities are used to build up the work of the church.

If you don't have an opportunity to invite people into your class, be prepared to name people who fill different positions in the church, what they do as part of their position, and how their talents help in the work of the church. Name some people your students may know, but also include people who are less visible to the public, such as people who deliver food baskets, work in the nursery, or clean the church.

Even though God has commanded us to love our brothers and sisters in the Lord, sometimes Christians have a hard time getting along. They don't cooperate. They may have different personalities, cultures, or ways of thinking. We learned how hard it is to cooperate when we built our marshmallow structure. It's even harder to cooperate in the church when we are working with so many different kinds of people. But it is the Holy Spirit's job to build the church. He helps us to get along with each other. We need to rely on His power to love each other and to work together.

One difference among Christians is that we all have different abilities and talents. Some of us are good teachers; others are good at doing the background helping. Some are pastors; others are good at singing. The church needs all different kinds of people to make it work the way it should.

At this point, tell students about others who work in the church, or, if you have invited people to class, allow the guests to talk about what they do for the church. Emphasize that no matter what specific tasks people do in the church, the ultimate goals are to tell others about Jesus and to teach believers more about the Bible.

In the early church, the leaders were different from each other. Peter and Paul were different in many ways. Let's look at some of these ways.

Draw the following chart on the board. Through a discussion with your students, fill in the boxes. Help your students see how these qualities (even if they may seem like negatives to us) were pluses in God's hands. The italicized material is suggested for your discussion.

DIFFERENCES	PETER	PAUL
Background	*(Fisherman, little education, came from Galilee)*	*(Jewish religious leader, well-educated, born in Tarsus)*
How he came into the church	*(Jesus called him and spent three years teaching him)*	*(Did not know Jesus before Jesus died; persecuted Christians before he believed in Jesus, then Jesus called him in a vision)*
Personality	*(Impatient, enthusiastic, impetuous, loyal)*	*(Determined, cultured, forceful, intelligent)*

Like Peter, after his vision of the sheet coming down from heaven, Paul had a plan on how he would preach the gospel. Let's read about it. **Read Romans 15:20.**

- Who did Paul want to tell about God's love and forgiveness? *(Those who had never heard about it before. People that other Christians were not ministering to.)*

So both Peter and Paul, the two most important leaders in the early church, wanted everyone to hear about Jesus. They tried to tell everyone they came into contact with about God's love and how Jesus came to earth to pay for our sins. In other words, Peter and Paul spent their lives helping to fulfill the Great Commission, the last command Jesus gave the new believers. Both Peter and Paul also spent lots of time teaching the new believers how to live for Jesus.

And this is the job we are given, too. We are responsible to help build up the church and to tell others about Jesus. We need to work together to help God's church.

APPLICATION: Working Together

Peter and Paul weren't alone when they were preaching and telling others about Jesus. The Holy Spirit was with them, helping them. The Holy Spirit is with us too. He's the One who makes it possible for us to use our talents and abilities to help build up the church.

You may think that you are too young to help build up the church. But that is not true. Every believer can help. The Holy Spirit has something for you to do that will fit your age and your abilities. The Holy Spirit will teach you as you do God's work. If you can sing, you could be in a children's choir. All of us can help keep our church clean by picking up trash and other litter. We can all be examples to the younger children in our church of how to be Christlike. And we can all tell others about Jesus.

Let's look at some ways the Holy Spirit can help us learn how to build up the church.

Divide your class into two groups. Give each person a pencil and a "What I Can Do" handout. Make sure each group has a Bible. Write the following verse references on the board: Acts 1:8; Acts 4:31; Acts 7:54–60; Acts 13:2–4.

In your group, look up the verses I have written on the board. Find one way the Holy Spirit helps us in each passage. Write that way down on your handouts. Your group will report what you found in a few minutes.

Give groups time to work. Circulate and help them find answers. When groups finish, gather as a class. Go over what the groups found. Some good answers are:

Acts 1:8—*(The Holy Spirit gives us power to be a witness for Jesus.)*

Acts 4:31—*(The Holy Spirit gives us boldness in telling others about Jesus.)*

Acts 7:54–60—*(The Holy Spirit gives us peace and confidence in difficult situations.)*

Acts 13:2–4—*(The Holy Spirit gives us guidance about the work He wants us to do.)*

Now that we have looked at what the Holy Spirit does to help us, let's write out a prayer that we can use when we do God's work.

With the students' help, write out a prayer on the board that incorporates all the elements in the verses above. The following is an example you can use to guide the discussion:

Dear heavenly Father,

I want to do your work by telling others about Jesus. I ask Your Holy Spirit to give me the power to do this. Please give me the boldness to talk to my friends about Jesus. Don't let me be afraid about what they might say that I won't like. Help me be kind and gentle and brave when I talk to them. Show me which people need to hear about

Your Son, Jesus, and show me when I should talk to them.

Thank You for giving me Your Holy Spirit to guide me.

In Jesus' name, amen.

When you finish, have students write the prayer on their handouts under the heading "A prayer I can use."

MEMORY VERSE ACTIVITY: Pass on the Message

Group 1—*"But you will receive power when the Holy Spirit comes upon you;*

Group 2—*and you will be my witnesses in Jerusalem,*

Group 3—*and in all Judea*

Group 4—*and Samaria,*

Group 5—*and to the ends of the earth." Acts 1:8*

Write the verse on the board as shown. Divide your class into five groups. Have students stand in a line in the order of their numbers (group 1 at one end of the line and group 5 at the other end). Give group 1 a Bible.

As we learned earlier, Jesus commands us to take His message of love and forgiveness to the whole world. Let's memorize our verse in a way that represents how we can do this. Group 1 is at the starting point. This is where the message starts—in each of our hearts. We hear the good news that Jesus died for our sins and ask Him to be our Savior. Group 1 will say the first part of the verse together. Then they will hand the Bible to group 2. That represents how we tell others about Jesus and give them the message of the gospel. Then group 2 will say the part of the verse that includes Jerusalem, which represents our city, and they will pass the Bible on to group 3. As soon as group 3 receives the Bible, they will say their part of the verse then hand the Bible to group 4, and so on.

We will follow this pattern until the Bible reaches group 5 and they say their part of the verse. That represents that the good news of Jesus Christ has gone to the ends of the earth. Then group 5 will walk to the front of the line and will become group 1. All the other groups will become the next highest group number. Then we will go through our verse again.

Keep rotating groups and going through the verse activity until your students know the verse. If desired, have individual students say the verse to you.

CHECK FOR UNDERSTANDING: Holy Spirit Help

Name each of the following references, and have students tell how the Holy Spirit has promised to help in each passage. (You do not need to read the verse since the students should have the answers on their "What Can I Do?" handouts.) Make sure the answers given below are mentioned. Then ask students to give an example of how the Holy Spirit could help them in each of the four ways.

Acts 1:8—*(power to witness)*

Acts 4:31—*(boldness in witnessing)*

Acts 7:54–60—*(peace and confidence in difficult situations)*

Acts 13:2–4—*(guidance in what to do for God)*

When you finish, have a student add the "Peter and Cornelius" picture to the time line to the right of the resurrection picture.

WEEKLY ASSIGNMENT: Sent Out to Work

This week students will be memorizing the Letters of Paul: Romans, 1 and 2 Corinthians, Galatians, Ephesians, Philippians, Colossians, 1 and 2 Thessalonians, 1 and 2 Timothy, Titus, and Philemon. Have students record this information in their Bible Reading Journals. Their daily reading assignments are as follows:

Day 1—Acts 1
Day 2—Acts 2
Day 3—Acts 3
Day 4—Acts 4
Day 5—Acts 5
Day 6—Acts 6
Day 7—Acts 7

Make sure students have their handouts and pencils. This week, let's see how we can work to help build up the church. Last week, you already started by telling someone about Jesus. Let's continue to do this. At the bottom of your handout, write the name of one person you would like to talk to this week about Jesus. Write that name under number 1. **Give students a moment to write.**

Now think of other things you could do to help build up our church. Some of these could be things you are doing right now, things you should start doing right now, or things you want to do in the future. You could write: Pick up trash on the church lawn. Clean up my classroom after class. Sing in the youth choir. Tell my little brother or sister some Bible stories. Send my pastor an encouraging note. There are many other things you could do. First, pray the prayer that you wrote earlier on your handout. Then write what you think God wants you to do. I'll give you some time to pray and write.

Give students time to pray and write. Then close in prayer, thanking God that He has included each of you in His worldwide church and that He has given you your local church. Ask God to help your students follow through on the work God has for them to do.

Take your handout home and use it this week. Pray the prayer and work on the jobs that you wrote down. Next week, we'll talk about what you did.

Peter and Cornelius

Peter's dream   Peter preaching at Cornelius's house

What I Can Do

The Holy Spirit will help me by giving me:

Acts 1:8

Acts 4:31

Acts 7:54–60

Acts 13:2–4

A prayer I can use:

Things I can do:

1. Tell others about Jesus. I am going to tell _____ about Jesus.

2. _____

3. _____

4. _____

The Church Grows

LESSON PLAN

OBJECTIVE: Students will see how the gospel is amplified and defined through the New Testament writers.

APPLICATION: Students will write a letter to someone asking for help in growing in Christ.

LESSON PLAN ELEMENT	ACTIVITY	TIME	SUPPLIES
Opening Activity	*Meet the Writers*	7–10	1 copy of "Meet the Writers" master; clothing for Bible actors
Bible Story—Assorted Scriptures; the main ideas of the New Testament writers	*What the Writers Wrote*	10–15	Bibles; paper; pencils; dry-erase marker or chalk
Lesson Activity	*Perfect Ingredients*	7–10	Bowl; plastic sandwich baggies; napkins; your students' favorite ingredients for trail mix; 1 copy of "The New Testament Writers" master
Check for Understanding	*Writer's Who's Who*	3–5	"The New Testament Writers" copy
Memory Verse Activity	*Growing by Learning*	3–5	Bowl; chocolate chips; dry-erase marker or chalk
Application	*Dear Friend*	7–10	Paper; pencil
Weekly Assignment	*Being Faithful*	3–5	Letters from Application

So far, we have divided the study of the New Testament into two parts—the Gospels, which tell of Christ's birth, life, death, and resurrection, and Acts, the beginning of the church. Now we will examine a third section of the New Testament—the books written to believers in specific churches about a new life in Christ. In the next lesson, we will conclude our study with future events as described by the book of Revelation.

Of the 27 books in the New Testament, 21 are letters. Thirteen of these letters are definitely written by Paul. Many scholars think he also wrote Hebrews. Other writers of the Epistles (letters) include Peter, James, John, and Jude.

God used Paul to write much of the New Testament. Paul was a Roman citizen, a Jew of Tarsus, a Hebrew of the Hebrews. He was brought up at the feet of a great teacher, Gamaliel, but became a missionary to Jesus Christ. From the day of his conversion, Paul's very life was summed up in his own words, "For to me, to live is Christ and to die is gain" (Philippians 1:21).

Ephesians, Philippians, Colossians, and Philemon are called the "Prison Epistles" because they were written by Paul during his first imprisonment mentioned in Acts 28. Ephesians, Philippians, and Colossians contain practical help for living out Christian principles. In Philemon, Paul encourages forgiveness for Philemon's slave, Onesimus, who may have stolen from his master before he ran away. Paul encourages believers everywhere to treat others with Christian love and fellowship. In his Thessalonian epistles, Paul assures believers at Thessalonica of the return of Jesus and corrects their misconceptions about the resurrection and the timing of the Second Coming of Christ. His letters focus on courage in the face of persecution and being prepared for Christ's return.

From the time of his first missionary journey, Paul always had co-workers. The "Pastoral Epistles" (1 and 2 Timothy and Titus) were written to those who were helping him to strengthen the churches he had founded.

The "General Epistles" (Hebrews; James; 1 and 2 Peter; 1, 2, 3 John; Jude) is an imperfect way to characterize the last eight epistles of the New Testament. That term has been selected because, unlike the majority of Paul's epistles that are written to specific churches, most of the recipients of these eight epistles are either a collection of churches or all the Christians of some large area (the exceptions are Hebrews and 2 and 3 John). Also, with the exception of Hebrews, these epistles are named for their authors. (Hebrews was given its name because it was originally addressed to Jewish Christians.)

The goal for this lesson is not to teach your students the content of each book but to give them an overview of what these books say. So don't get bogged down in details but concentrate on the bigger picture.

LESSON PLAN

OPENING ACTIVITY: Meet the Writers

Before Class: Collect clothing that your students can wear to act the parts of Paul, Peter, James, John, and Jude. You could use cloths to drape over heads, robes that look like shepherds' clothing, and scarves to drape over shoulders.

Also, cut apart the Personality Scripts on the "Meet the Writers" copy.

Ask the students to name a person with whom they shared their faith this week and what they did to help build up the church. Comment on how many different ways your students have named for building up the church. Talk about how the Holy Spirit fits together all our abilities to make the church grow.

Select five students to read the parts of Paul, Peter, James, John, and Jude. If you have a small class, eliminate the roles of James and Jude. Give students the clothing they are to wear and the Personality Script from the "Meet the Writers" copy. Instruct actors to read over their scripts and be prepared to read the part of the person they represent. Encourage them to read their scripts with a lot of emotion.

Today, we have five people who have come to visit us. They lived long ago, and now they want to tell us their story. Each of them wrote at least one book of the Bible.

One at a time, have actors read their scripts. When they finish, lead the following discussion:

- Why did these writers write their books? *(To tell others about Jesus; to warn believers about false teachers; to help Christians in the new churches; to tell what was going to happen in the future.)*

- How did they write their books? *(The Holy Spirit gave each one the exact words to write down. That is what is meant when we say that the Bible is divinely inspired.)*

- Who wrote the most books? *(Paul.)*

- Who wrote the last book of the Bible? *(John.)*

From the beginning to the end of the New Testament, the message is the same: Jesus Christ came to die for our sins. When we accept His sacrifice on our behalf, we become children of God and God then helps us live holy and joyful lives. Isn't that a great message?

BIBLE STORY: What the Writers Wrote

The New Testament writers suffered for Jesus. They were put in prison, beaten, and called names. Paul was shipwrecked. Many, including Peter, were killed for their faith. But even when they faced persecution, they never gave up. They wanted to tell more and more people

about Jesus, build up the new believers in their faith, start new churches, and teach the people in the churches, especially the leaders.

Let's look at some of the things that they considered important.

Form five groups and give each group paper and a pencil. Make sure each group has a Bible.

The writers of the New Testament books, not including the Gospels and Acts, wrote for these reasons. **Write the reasons on the board.**

1. To tell people how to become Christians

2. To warn about wrong teachings

3. To build up believers in their faith

4. To teach leaders of new churches they started

Assign your groups these books:

Group 1—Romans, 1 and 2 Corinthians
Group 2— Galatians, Ephesians, Philippians, and Colossians
Group 3—1 and 2 Thessalonians, 1 and 2 Timothy, Titus, and Philemon
Group 4—Hebrews, James, 1 and 2 Peter
Group 5—1, 2, 3 John, Jude, and Revelation

Have groups write the names of their assigned New Testament books on their sheet of paper.

In your group, skim through the books you were assigned. Do *not* read each verse. See if you can find one verse to go along with each of the four reasons on the board. Write down the reference to that verse after the number of the reason.

Give groups five to ten minutes to work. Circulate, helping each group. The goal is to help students become familiar with the books, not to come up with the best answers. If groups are having problems coming up with verses, help them by giving them some to look up. Some possibilities are:

1. Romans 5:1; Ephesians 2:8,9; 1 Thessalonians 2:13; 2 Peter 3:9; 1 John 5:1

2. 1 Corinthians 1:10–17; Galatians 1:6–9; 2 Thessalonians 2:1–4; Hebrews 13:9,10; 2 John 7

3. 2 Corinthians 1:3; Philippians 2:12,13; 2 Timothy 2:2; 1 Peter 5:1–3; 1 John 4:7

4. 1 Corinthians 1:1,2; Colossians 1:1,2; 1 Timothy 1:1,2; James 1:1,2; Jude 1,2

When finished, have a member of each group read their verses as you write their answers on the board.

Then give these interesting facts:

• We don't know who wrote the book of Hebrews, but many Bible scholars think Paul did.

- Paul wrote Ephesians, Philippians, Colossians, and Philemon while he was in prison the first time. (He was in prison many times.)

- Paul wrote 1 and 2 Timothy and Titus to pastors to help them lead their churches.

- Stories tell us that when the Romans crucified Peter, he asked to be crucified upside down because he didn't feel he was good enough to die the same way Jesus did.

- Because people didn't like the fact that John preached about Jesus, he was sent to the island of Patmos where he lived until he died.

You can see that the writers of the New Testament were all faithful to Jesus Christ. They obeyed God and taught many others how to live for the Lord.

LESSON ACTIVITY: Perfect Ingredients

Before Class: Purchase ingredients to make a delicious trail mix. Bring at least five ingredients, such as peanuts, raisins, dried fruit, Chex cereal, toasted oats cereal, pretzels, or M&Ms. Place each ingredient in a separate plastic baggie.

Have students sit around a table. Give each person a sandwich-size baggie. Set the bowl in the middle of the table.

Have you ever eaten trail mix? Trail mix is a nutritious food that people often take on a hike or campout. It is a quick source of energy, easy to carry, and fun to eat. Let's make some trail mix.

Have students put their baggies over their hands so they can stir the mix. Add the ingredients a little at a time, allowing each person a turn at mixing. When finished, have students put napkins in front of themselves and take a handful of trail mix to eat while you discuss the activity.

Trail mix has a variety of ingredients, but it's all good. It is nutritious because we put in the right ingredients. It tastes good because we put in delicious things. Isn't that like the books of the Bible? There are so many different books, written by different authors, yet it is all one message.

- How are the ideas put in the New Testament by the writers like our trail mix? *(Everything that was added is good for us. The Bible has lots of ideas, but they're all good. The Bible has the right ingredients.)*

- Why do you think God used so many writers to give us the New Testament? *(Because then the New Testament would have lots of different ideas and ways of thinking about them. God wanted to show us that His Word is for many different kinds of people.)*

God had many things to tell the new churches. He had principles He wanted them to learn. So God used all these different writers to get His message across to the believers and the new churches that were being started in so many places. These are the writers the Holy

Spirit used to write the books in the New Testament after Acts: **Point out each writer from the "The New Testament Writers" as you say his name.** Paul, Peter, John, James, and Jude.

The Holy Spirit used each writer in a different way. Paul didn't write like Peter. Peter didn't write like James. They each wrote to different churches or groups of people. And yet God's Spirit made sure that the words they wrote down were all perfect, right, and good.

Just like we might take trail mix on a trip to give us nutrition and energy, we need the Bible to help us walk through our Christian life.

The New Testament writers teach us about God's message to us. In this message are several main ideas. Let's think about these. **Write the italicized points on the board as you give them.**

1. *How a person can become a Christian.* The most important teaching in the New Testament is how a person can become a Christian. Paul writes in Romans that we are all sinners and need a Savior. He tells us that we are saved by faith, not good works. The other writers also tell us this same principle. You can find the truth of how to become a Christian all the way through the New Testament.

2. *How we must grow as Christians.* Another main idea in the New Testament is that we must grow in our spiritual lives. The writers give us many truths about how to grow, such as reading the Bible, following Christ's example, meeting regularly with other believers to stay on track, praying all the time, and many others.

3. *That God must be most important in our lives.* We cannot let anyone or anything like money or toys take God's first place in our lives. If we do, we will fall into sin and dishonor God's name. We must stay true to God for the rest of our lives.

4. *That we must avoid sin and confess our sin when we do fall short of God's standards.* God wants us to deal with the sin in our lives. If we don't, we won't obey Him and we won't have joyful lives.

5. *That we must witness about Jesus Christ to people around us.* God has given us the greatest gift we could ever receive—eternal life in Jesus. Therefore, we must share our faith with others so that they too can find this greatest gift.

- Which one of these principles do you think Christians have the most trouble obeying? *(Avoiding sin because we all do wrong things. Witnessing because it's hard to tell people about Jesus if they don't want to hear. Making God first in our lives because we are tempted to make money or toys more important than God.)*

Each one of us may have a different answer to this question. And at certain times in your life, one may be harder to obey than the others. But God has given us many wonderful verses in the Bible to help us with the problem areas we are facing. That's why it's so important to keep reading and studying the New Testament. God will help you with any problem area you have.

God's Holy Spirit is the answer to our problems. He wrote the Bible. That makes every word in the Bible perfect and true. Then the Holy Spirit helps us obey God's Word. The Holy Spirit is the key to our Christian growth.

CHECK FOR UNDERSTANDING: Writer's Who's Who

Have students sit in a circle. Have a student put "The New Testament Writers" picture on the time line after the "Peter and Cornelius" picture.

Ask individual students to call out a book of the Bible from Romans to Revelation. You tell them who wrote the book and point out the writer's picture on the time line. (For Hebrews say, "Perhaps Paul did," or, "We don't know.") Next, you call out the name of a book of the New Testament. Have the first person in the circle name the writer of that book. (You could also have the student come up and point out the picture on the time line.) For example, if you called out "Romans" the first person should say "Paul." As you name the next book in sequence, have the next student in the circle name the writer. Continue this way around the circle. Students may need to go through the books of the Bible a couple of times before they readily recognize who wrote each one. You may include the Gospels and Acts in this activity if you desire, but there are no drawings for Matthew, Mark, and Luke.

If you have time, call out the name of a writer and have a student tell one fact about that person.

MEMORY VERSE ACTIVITY: Growing by Learning

Colossians 2:6,7—"So then, just as you received Christ Jesus as Lord, continue to live in him, rooted and built up in him, strengthened in the faith as you were taught, and overflowing with thankfulness."

Optional Activity: If you want to wait to eat the trail mix until now, use pieces of the trail mix for this activity instead of chocolate chips. Use the napkins and baggies at this time.

Write the verse on the board. Read it aloud. Have students sit around a table near the board. This verse tells about our Christian life. First we ask Jesus to be our Savior and Lord. Then we live our Christian life by being strengthened in our faith as the New Testament writers and our friends and teachers have taught us. As we are taught, God wants us to be thankful for Jesus, for what we are learning and how we are growing in our spirits.

Let's learn this verse to help us remember to grow in Christ.

Set out a bowl with chocolate chips. Go around the circle, having each person say one word of the verse. Each student who says the word correctly may take a chocolate chip and eat it. When you have gone around the circle a couple of times, erase the verse from the board and try it again.

When you finish, go around the circle once more, having the students give a thank-you for something they have learned from God's Word.

APPLICATION: Dear Friend

It is very important to grow in Christ. That's what the New Testament writers tell us.

- What are some ways that people your age can grow in Christ? *(By reading the Bible every day and doing what you read about. Praying all the time. Studying the Ten Commandments and obeying them. Helping others even when it's not convenient. Going to church every week. Memorizing Bible verses.)*

- Why is it so important for someone your age to grow in Christ? *(God wants us to grow in Christ. Because we have the rest of our lives to serve Jesus. If we develop good ways of living now, we will not have as many problems later.)*

Growing in Christ means listening to God's Word and obeying it. The New Testament writers give us many things we should do to become more like Jesus. They want us to grow in Christ.

We all need help in doing what's right. I do and you do. Unless we ask the Holy Spirit to help us do what's right, we will fail. And God wants us to be with other Christians who will also help us do what's right.

Distribute paper and pencils. Make sure your five points from the Lesson Activity are still written on the board.

We all need friends who will help us to grow in Christ and become more like Jesus. Today we will write a letter to a friend, describing our relationship with Jesus. First, think of a person who helps you grow in Christ. It could be a parent, a grandparent, someone else—or even me—a person who is interested in your spiritual growth. When you're finished, you will give the letter to that person.

Give students a moment to think.

A letter starts with a greeting, such as "Dear Grandma" or "Dear Jason." Write a greeting using the person's name at the top of your paper and put a comma after the greeting.

Give students a moment to write their greetings.

Below the greeting, write several lines explaining how you became a Christian. You might write something like this: "Just after my 8th birthday, I asked Jesus to be my Savior. I was at home with my dad and he helped me pray and ask God to forgive my sins."

Give students time to think and write. Encourage those who are having trouble coming up with something. If you have students who have never asked Jesus to be their Savior, have a children's evangelistic booklet ready to review with them and do not have those students complete the letter. (See the Resources for information on how to order the booklet *Would You Like to Belong to God's Family?*)

Now write a new paragraph in your letter. Write one specific way you want to grow in Christ. Ask the person to whom you addressed the letter to help you grow in this way. You might write something like this: "I want to be kinder to my little sister. Sometimes I yell at her. I will ask the Holy Spirit to help me be kind whenever I start getting mad. Instead of getting mad when she bugs me, I will walk away. Will you help me during the next week by praying for me and asking me if I am making progress on being kinder?"

Give students time to think and write.

A letter always ends with a closing. Below your last paragraph, write a closing such as "Sincerely" or "Your friend" with a comma after it. Then sign your name below the closing.

Give students time to do this.

Aren't you glad that the Bible teaches us so many ways to do what's right and to keep our lives pure? God used the New Testament writers to give us His message. They were faithful to do what God asked them to do. We can be faithful just like they were.

WEEKLY ASSIGNMENT: Being Faithful

This week students will be memorizing the "General Epistles": Hebrews; James; 1 and 2 Peter; 1, 2, and 3 John; and Jude.

In their Bible Reading Journals, have students record their daily reading assignments:

Day 1—Romans 12
Day 2—1 Corinthians 13
Day 3—2 Corinthians 5
Day 4—Galatians 6
Day 5—Ephesians 2
Day 6—Philippians 2
Day 7—Colossians 3

We have learned a lot about the Bible. We learned about the Old Testament and Bible characters such as Moses, Joshua, and Elijah. They were all faithful to do what God asked them to do. We've learned about Jesus and what He came to do. And last, we've learned about New Testament believers who were faithful even when they endured persecution and hard trials.

Let's be like them. Let's be faithful too. Take your letter to the person to whom you wrote it. Over the next week, have that person help you do what you said you wanted to do in the letter. We'll hear about what happened next week in our class time.

Close in prayer, asking the Holy Spirit to help your students follow through on what they wrote in their letters. Then thank God for giving us the New Testament.

Meet the Writers

Paul

My name is Paul. I was born in Tarsus into an important Jewish family. I studied the Jewish faith from a famous teacher named Gamaliel. When I first learned about the Christians, I tried to get rid of them. In fact, I was there when some people stoned Stephen to death. Then later, the risen Jesus met me on the road to Damascus. Right then, I realized that I had been persecuting the Son of God. I became a believer and started preaching the gospel in every place I went. I became a missionary for Jesus.

With the Holy Spirit's help, I wrote 13 letters to churches that I started. They became books of the Bible. I wrote these letters to teach people how to become a Christian, how to solve problems in the church, how to live as a Christian, and how pastors should lead their people.

I wrote some of my letters from prison. I was put in prison because of my preaching for Jesus. But while I was in prison, I told people about Jesus and kept working for my Lord.

Peter

I was one of Jesus' twelve disciples. You may remember that I was the one who denied Jesus when He was arrested. After I realized what I had done, I felt so bad that I didn't think Jesus would ever want to have anything to do with me again. But on the day Jesus was resurrected, He appeared to me and talked to me. I knew then that Jesus had forgiven me for what I had done. Then I wanted to serve Him with all my heart.

I wrote two books of the Bible, 1 and 2 Peter. I was writing to many churches scattered throughout Asia Minor. I wanted to strengthen Christians so they could stand firm against the terrible persecutions that they were suffering in the Roman Empire.

James

I am the half brother of Jesus. (Since Jesus didn't have an earthly father, we don't have the same father, but we both have the same mother, Mary.) I was not one of the twelve disciples, but I became a leader in the Jerusalem church after Jesus went back to heaven.

I wrote one book of the Bible that is called by my name, James. In it, I reminded Christians about how their hearts and lives should be totally devoted to Jesus and that they should not follow wrong teachings. I wanted people to know how they can have joy in Christ even when they are suffering for His sake.

John

I too was one of the disciples. I was the one that Jesus said He loved. When He was arrested, I ran away, but followed at a distance to see what happened. I was not brave enough to stand up for my Lord when He needed me. During my later years, I lived in Ephesus among Christians who had trusted in Christ when Paul preached in our city. While I was there, a false teacher became popular who said that living a holy life was not important. I wrote to tell the people that his ideas were wrong.

I wrote five books of the Bible: the Gospel of John; 1, 2, and 3 John; and Revelation. I wrote 1 John to argue against the bad teaching that the false teacher had spread among the Christians. I also told believers that they could be sure that they have eternal life. I wrote 2 John to help people love other Christians. My other book, 3 John, was written to church leaders who went from town to town helping new churches. They depended on the hospitality of other believers. I was thanking these believers for opening their homes and for being faithful to care for the church leaders who were so far from home. Revelation is all about what will happen in the future when Jesus comes again. Many of the things I wrote in that book are so mysterious that I didn't understand what I was writing. I just wrote down what the Holy Spirit wanted me to say.

Jude

I was another one of Jesus' half brothers. I did not believe He was God until after the resurrection, so I did not get the privilege of being one of His disciples. And I was not one of the official apostles either. But I am so glad that I recognized that Jesus is the Christ, the Son of God, and that I can serve Him.

I wrote one book of the Bible, which is called by my name, Jude. I warned believers about false Christians who had slipped into the church and who wanted to change the message of Jesus. I also wanted the believers to continue in their faith and not give up. I warned the churches about false teachers who were trying to lead the believers astray.

The New Testament Writers

Jude Peter James John Paul

LESSON 12

The End of the Story

LESSON PLAN

OBJECTIVE: Students will learn about future events as given in the Book of Revelation.

APPLICATION: Students will prepare for the coming of Christ.

LESSON PLAN ELEMENT	ACTIVITY	TIME	SUPPLIES
Opening Activity	*Role-Playing Roles*	10–15	Charades role-play props (see activity); 3 index cards; marker or pen
Bible Story—Revelation 1:9–20, the Second Coming of Jesus	*The Conquering King*	7–10	Bibles; dry-erase marker or chalk; paper; markers
Lesson Activity	*The King Returns*	7–10	Bibles; 8 slips of paper; pen; 1 copy of "The Future and the King" master
Memory Verse Activity	*Hurrah! Jesus Is Coming!*	3–5	Dry-erase marker or chalk
Application	*Ready and Waiting*	7–10	"Ready and Waiting" handouts; pencils
Check for Understanding	*From Beginning to End*	3–5	Complete time line and all pictures, including "The Future and the King"; tape
Weekly Assignment	*Are You Waiting for Jesus?*	3–5	"Ready and Waiting" handouts; pencils; the 8 questions from the Lesson Activity

The last book in the New Testament is the record of the revelation that the apostle John received while he was imprisoned on the island of Patmos for being a Christian. Many of the chapters of this books are difficult to interpret. Some of the greatest theologians in the history of the Church have felt unequal to the task of expounding these Scriptures. For example, John Calvin, one of the great reformers, wrote a commentary on every book of the Bible except Revelation.

Despite the fact that the meaning may not be immediately apparent for every part of the book, there is the promise that those who take it to heart will be blessed (1:3).

Although some parts may be obscure, certain ideas do stand out with unquestioned clarity. Chapters 1 through 3 describe Jesus as He appeared to John and record His messages to the seven churches of Asia Minor. These messages are quite clear in their meaning. Chapters 4 through 18 are more difficult but chapters 19 through 22, which concern those events by which God brings final redemption to the world, are clear for the most part. These four chapters are extremely important to completing the history of redemption outlined since Genesis.

Recently, Christians everywhere have been reading books—both fiction and nonfiction —about future events. Some of these books have been rewritten for elementary age readers. If you can obtain a few, you may want to bring them to class and get your students interested in reading them.

Most children have a limited understanding of the future because they have not lived very long and so they cannot put the future into perspective. However, your students will be studying American and world history in their school classrooms so they are beginning to grasp the scope of history. This is where your time line comes into play. As you put the final drawing up, emphasize that no one except God knows the exact time that all these events will take place. But also show your excitement at the fact that Jesus may return at any moment.

LESSON PLAN

OPENING ACTIVITY: Role-Playing Roles

Before Class: Think of three sets of roles that people may have, such as mother/ doctor/gardener; father/Sunday School teacher/fireman; student/soccer team member/big brother or sister. Write each set on an index card. Bring a prop that goes with each of the different roles. For mother/doctor/gardener you could bring an apron, a stethoscope or lab coat, and gardening gloves. These items will be used in a game of charades, so make sure they will point students to the right role or job.

Discuss the ways that your students plan to grow in Christ. Talk about how the person to whom they wrote the letter helped them with their goal. Emphasize how important it is to enlist others to help us be more faithful to Jesus.

Have you ever thought about the many different kinds of roles you play in your life? You might be a cousin, a basketball player, and a son—all at the same time. Or you might be a daughter, an honor student, and a babysitter. In each role, you act differently and you do different things. You are the same person, but you have different jobs to do.

- What changes do you make between your role as a student at school and your role as a son or daughter at home? (*I act crazier at school than at home. At school I am quieter and at home I am noisier. At school I wear good clothes and at home I wear grubby clothes.*)

- Why do you change your behavior from one place to another? (*People expect me to act differently in different places. At school, I have to sit quietly at a desk and at home I can talk and turn the TV up loud. My friends encourage me to be funnier and my parents think I act too goofy, so I act crazier with my friends than with my parents.*)

Divide your class into three groups. All people act differently in different roles. This is true with both adults and children. Let's act out some roles people may have. I will give each group a card with three roles on it. These three roles can be a part of one person's life. In your group, decide how you will act out these roles. You will act out the roles in front of the other two groups. Let's see if the other groups can guess what you are acting out.

Set out the props and let groups choose what they want to use. Give groups time to decide how to act out their roles. Then have each group act out its roles and have the other groups guess what the roles are. Compliment the groups for their acting.

Now that we have thought about the different roles that each of us may play in life, we can see that roles may change how we look, how we act, and what we do.

- What are some roles that you expect to play in the future that you cannot do now? (*I want to be a pilot but I've never flown a plane before. I want to be a wife and a mother one day. I can hardly wait until I'm a high school student.*)

- How long will it take before you can play that role? (*I have three more years until I'm in high school. Becoming a pilot takes a lot of training so it may be fifteen more years. I want to wait until I'm out of college to get married.*)

- Can you think of some people in the Bible who played different roles? (*Moses was a shepherd and a leader. Peter was a disciple and an apostle. Paul persecuted Christians and then he became a preacher for Jesus.*)

Jesus has different roles also. In our Bible Story, we'll learn about a role that Jesus has not played yet. It is coming in the future and I am very excited about it.

BIBLE STORY: The Conquering King

First, let's think about the role that Jesus played when He lived on earth. What did He look like? What did He do? Where did He go?

Write the heading "Jesus on earth" on one side of the board. Have students think of what Jesus was like when He lived on earth. Write these ideas on the board as students mention them. Bring out what He might have looked like, how He lived an "ordinary" life (as opposed to the heavenly life He is living now), the places He went, and what people thought of Him. Some ideas are:

He looked like an ordinary man. He wore ordinary clothes. He lived in a regular house.

He walked around the Sea of Galilee to Jerusalem. Sometimes he rode on a donkey or sailed in a boat.

Lots of people didn't think He was anyone special. Other people thought He was the Messiah.

The apostle John wrote the last book of the Bible. It is called Revelation. **Point out the book in your Bible.** The revelation in this book is that of Jesus Christ the King. Jesus has changed since He lived on this earth. When He was born in a stable in Bethlehem, He put aside His glory, in the same way you would put away a beautiful piece of clothing if you went someplace where it might get dirty. Then after He arose from the dead, the Father gave Him all His glory back. Jesus does not look now like He looked when He was on the earth as a man. Let's read about it in Revelation.

Divide students into pairs. (If some students have trouble reading, pair them with students who are good readers.) Pass out a piece of paper to each pair. Make available a variety of colored markers. Read Revelation 1:9–20 with your partner. This is the description of Jesus that John saw in a vision. On your paper, draw what you think Jesus looks like according to John's vision.

Give students time to read and draw. Then have pairs share what they drew.

How would you like to have been the apostle John at that moment? He saw something that Christians had never seen before. The sight was so awesome that John could not perfectly describe Jesus in our language. The sight was so glorious that John fell over as if he were dead. As a human being, he could not bear to look on the awesome face of Jesus Christ.

Look at what Jesus said about Himself. **Read Revelation 1:17,18.** Jesus is the First and the Last. He was before creation and He will be after creation. He is everlasting. He was once dead but now He lives forever. He has all power so He holds the keys to death and Hades. The way John saw Jesus in his vision was very different from the way John saw Him when Jesus lived on the earth.

- How do you feel about the picture of Jesus as given by John in Revelation? (*He seems a little scary. I can't wait to see what He looks like. He certainly is different than when He was a baby in Bethlehem!*)

- What amazes you most about the description of Jesus in Revelation? (*His voice is like rushing water so it must be very loud or very musical. His eyes glowed like fire! He could hold seven stars at once. A sword came out of His mouth.*)

- What is different between the picture of Jesus in the Gospels (Matthew, Mark, Luke, and John) and the one in Revelation? (*Jesus shows His power in the Revelation picture but He hid much of His power in the Gospels picture. John was Jesus' disciple and walked around with Him all the time, but in Revelation, Jesus was so awesome looking that John fell over like he was dead.*)

When Jesus lived on earth, He came to die on a cross. He hid His power because He was going to pay for the sins of the people. He had to be a man to do that. He had no weapons. He did not fight. He let men kill Him on a cross.

But in Revelation, Jesus comes back to earth as the conquering King. This will happen in the future on a day that only God knows. Then Jesus will show all people His strength, wisdom, might, and glory. Did you notice that a sword came out of His mouth? That means that He will judge all the people for their sins.

The Book of Revelation has many mysteries in it. Many of the things described about the future even Bible scholars don't understand. Other events in Revelation are very clear. We will be learning about these events that will happen in the future. In this lesson, we will see what Jesus commanded John to write. Jesus has some commands for us, too. It is important that we learn and obey these commands.

LESSON ACTIVITY: The King Returns

 Before Class: Write each of the following references and questions on a separate slip of paper.

1. Revelation 19:11–13: Who is coming back to earth and what does He look like?
2. Revelation 19:14–16: What will Jesus do when He returns to earth?
3. Revelation 19:19: What do the wicked nations try to do?
4. Revelation 20:1–3: What will happen to the devil at the beginning of the reign of the King?

5. Revelation 20:7–10: What will happen to the devil after the thousand-year reign of Jesus Christ?

6. Revelation 20:11–15: What will happen to all those who have rejected Jesus as their Savior?

7. Revelation 21:1,2: What will come down from heaven for the believers?

8. Revelation 21:3–5: What will happen to the believers?

Cut apart the pictures from "The Future and the King" copy.

We have all heard or read many different kinds of stories—real life events, make-believe tales, mysteries, action thrillers. Let's see if you can think of some beginnings and endings of famous stories.

Allow volunteers to tell just the beginning and ending of stories. Students can draw from stories such as fairy tales, mystery novels, adventure series, books they've read, or movies they've seen. See if the other students can guess what each story is. Because the point of the activity is to emphasize beginnings and endings, make sure the story segments are short.

• How many of these stories had "happily ever after" endings? *(Allow volunteers to share.)*

The Bible has all of these kinds of stories in it. We have learned about many real-life events such as the lives of Adam and Eve, Moses, the prophets, and the apostles. We read about mysteries that the prophets foretold when they described how Jesus would be born and what would happen to Him. We saw how these mysteries were revealed when Jesus walked on this earth. We also read about some prophecies yet to come such as the Messiah returning to earth as a King. And we saw lots of action—Elijah calling fire down from heaven; Moses opening the Red Sea; Jesus raising from the dead.

We also read about the beginning of the story, the start of history when God created heaven and earth and Adam and Eve. But what about the end of the story? How will history on earth end? Will it have a "happily ever after" ending?

Of course, God is eternal so He has no beginning and no end. But human history has a beginning and an end. Adam and Eve were at the beginning. Jesus' Second Coming will be at the end. Let's look at some final events.

Give out the slips of paper with references on them to students who can read well. Ask students to read the verses silently and answer the question on their slip of paper. Give these students a minute or two to read and think. Then, starting with number 1, have them answer their questions. Bring out the points in italic as you discuss each question.

1. Revelation 19:11–13: Who is coming back to earth and what does He look like? *(This Person is Jesus Christ, the Word of God. The description of Him is similar to the one in Revelation chapter 1.)*

2. Revelation 19:14–16: What will Jesus do when He returns to earth? *(He will bring armies with Him. He will strike down the wicked nations. He will be the King of kings*

and the Lord of lords.)

3. Revelation 19:19: What do the wicked nations try to do? *(They try to defeat the army of Jesus. Explain that when Jesus defeats His enemies, He will reign on the earth for a thousand years.)*

4. Revelation 20:1–3: What will happen to the devil at the beginning of the reign of the King? *(He will be chained for a thousand years and thrown into the abyss, a bottomless pit.)*

5. Revelation 20:7–10: What will happen to the devil after the thousand-year reign of Jesus Christ? *(He will be thrown into the lake of fire.)*

6. Revelation 20:11–15: What will happen to all those who have rejected Jesus as their Savior? *(They will be judged and join the devil in the lake of fire.)*

7. Revelation 21:1,2: What will come down from heaven for the believers? *(A holy city of Jerusalem.)*

8. Revelation 21:3–5: What will happen to the believers? *(God will live with them forever. They will not have any more death or crying or pain. Everything will be made new.)*

Isn't this wonderful? **Show the picture of the Second Coming from "The Future and the King" copy.** It is a "happily ever after" ending! Jesus will defeat the devil and all his forces. Then Jesus will reign as the King of the earth for a thousand years. After the thousand years, the devil and his forces will try to defeat Jesus one more time. But of course, the devil can't win. Jesus will defeat the devil and throw him into the lake of fire forever.

Then a new city will come down from heaven for us believers to live in. God will live with us forever and ever. We will never have any pain or sorrow or death. It will be glorious! This is the end of the story that God has planned for those who love Him. Aren't you glad you are a Christian?

MEMORY VERSE ACTIVITY: Hurrah! Jesus Is Coming!

Revelation 21:6—"He said to me: 'It is done. I am the Alpha and the Omega, the Beginning and the End. To him who is thirsty I will give to drink without cost from the spring of the water of life.'"

Write the verse on the board. Read the verse aloud. In this verse, Jesus is speaking to John, and of course, to us as well. When Jesus says, "It is done," He is talking about His work of dying on the cross. When He says, "I will give to drink without cost from the spring of the water of life," He is telling us that any person on earth can have eternal life and that this life is a free gift because of the price Jesus paid when He sacrificed Himself on the cross.

Divide your class into two "cheerleading" groups. Today, we are going to cheer for Jesus and His promises to us. In your group, plan a cheer you can give using the memory verse. Your cheer can be dramatic with actions or it can use choreography like a sports cheering team. Just make sure that everyone in your group memorizes and says the verse aloud and participates in the actions.

Give groups time to plan. Then have each group give its "cheer." The "cheering" group should stand with their backs to the board so they can't see the verse. That way, you'll know if each student has memorized the verse. The other group should "cheer" the verse along with the "acting" group.

If you choose, have individuals say the verse to you.

APPLICATION: Ready and Waiting
Distribute the "Ready and Waiting" handouts and pencils.

Not only is Jesus coming again to wage war against the devil and his forces, but Jesus is also coming to take all the believers to heaven. This will happen before the Second Coming when Jesus comes on His white steed.

Jesus will not come all the way to earth to take the believers to heaven. He will meet us in the air. We will instantly fly up to meet Him. This event is called the Rapture. **Show the picture of the Rapture from "The Future and the King" copy.** This is a very important moment in church history. Then we will go to heaven with Jesus and celebrate a wedding supper with Him. The Bible says that the church (all believers) are the bride and Jesus is the groom. It will be a glorious event.

After the supper and other wonderful things, we will return with Jesus for His Second Coming to the earth. Then all the people on earth will know that Jesus is the Messiah. All the Jewish people on earth will see their King and will believe in Jesus. Jesus will come to fight on their behalf.

If you have brought children's books about future events, show them now. Explain that many believers are very excited about Jesus' return and that they want to read about what will happen in the future. Emphasize that many of the events portrayed in these books are ideas the author has about the future after reading the Bible.

No one knows for sure how all these future events will take place. Only God knows. But we can read Revelation and get some ideas of what Jesus will do.

In fact, the Bible tells us that no one knows the exact time or day when Jesus will come for His church (this means all the believers in the world). He will surprise us. That's why He wants to us be ready and waiting for His return. He wants us to be growing spiritually and to be doing the work He has given us to do. We will not have a chance to prepare when we see Him coming. He will come so fast that it will be like the twinkling of an eye. If we are not prepared, we will have to meet Him just the way we are. Let's make sure we are all ready and waiting for His return.

Look at the chart on your handout. On the chart are the names of seven churches. Jesus gave commands to seven churches that were serving God when John wrote the Book of Revelation. They are found in Revelation chapters 2 and 3. The commands to these seven churches are for us today, too.

In the third church, to "repent" means to be sorry for your sins and change your ways. In the sixth church, Laodicea, being lukewarm means not serving God with your whole heart but just obeying Him a little. It's like drinking hot chocolate when it's just barely warm. It doesn't taste good. God wants our feelings for Him to be hot. While we wait for the Rapture, Jesus wants us to be doing His work. After each command, write one way you can obey the command in your life.

Give students time to fill out the chart. Students will tend to give general answers, so circulate and help them decide on specific answers. Below are some examples of answers your students could give to the commands.

COMMAND TO THE CHURCH	HOW I WILL OBEY THE COMMAND
The church in Ephesus: Keep your love for God fresh.	*(I will read the Bible every day and go to church every week. I will tell Jesus I love Him every day.)*
The church in Smyrna: Be faithful during trials.	*(Whenever something bad happens to me, I will still follow Jesus' commands. When kids tease me at school, I won't say bad words back. I'll be nice to them.)*
The church in Pergamum: Repent of your sins.	*(I will tell God I'm sorry when I do something wrong. Each time I slip and tell a lie, I will say I'm sorry to God and the person I lied to. I'll also tell that person the truth.)*
The church in Thyatira: Keep My commandments.	*(I will review the Ten Commandments frequently to make sure I am keeping them. I will note the commandment I am having the most trouble with and work on that one. I will write down the commands I read about in my daily Bible reading and follow those commands.)*
The church in Sardis: Keep yourself pure from wrongdoing.	*(Whenever anyone tries to influence me to do something wrong like cheat on a test, I will say "No!")*
The church in Laodicea: Be zealous for God, not lukewarm.	*(I will not hide my love for God. I will tell others about Him and how much I love Him.)*
The church in Philadelphia: Keep God's Word.	*(In my daily Bible reading, I will write down things I should do to keep God's Word, like thanking God or loving others. Then I will follow through and do these things.)*

CHECK FOR UNDERSTANDING: From Beginning to End

Tape the picture of the Rapture from "The Future and the King" on the time line. To the right of that, tape the picture of the King's Second Coming. Then have eight volunteers put the numbered questions from the Lesson Activity under this picture in order (1 through 8). As each student tapes up a question, have him or her briefly explain the answer.

Review the story of man from the beginning to the end, bringing out the different eras: creation, the Patriarchs, the nation of Israel, the coming of Jesus, the beginning of the church, and the future coming of Jesus. Ask:

- Who is the central Person of the Bible? (*Jesus Christ.*)

- Why is He so important? (*He is God. He came to save us from our sins. He created us and He loves us.*)

WEEKLY ASSIGNMENT: Are You Waiting for Jesus?

Have students review the General Epistles and add the Book of Revelation.

Instruct students to record their daily reading assignments in their Bible Reading Journals:

Day 1—Revelation 1
Day 2—Revelation 2
Day 3—Revelation 3
Day 4—Revelation 19
Day 5—Revelation 20
Day 6—Revelation 21
Day 7—Revelation 22

Underneath your chart, you will find three questions. Answer them very carefully. They are for your eyes only, so don't show them to anyone else.

Give students time to think and write. After a few moments, explain to your students how excited you are about the return of Jesus. Tell them what you are doing to prepare for His coming.

Then let the students share their ideas of what they want to do to prepare for the Lord's coming. The following are some ideas you might suggest:

- Talk to Jesus more often.

- Make sure you don't have any sin in your life.

- Get up every morning thinking, *This may be the day that Jesus comes back.*

- Tell your friends who are not believers about Jesus and how they can be forgiven.

- Tell other friends who are believers about "The End of the Story" in the Bible.

- **Praise God that all His promises will come true, especially that Jesus will come back for His people.**

When you get home, post this chart in your bedroom. Obey the commands you wrote in the chart. Let the chart remind you that Jesus has promised to return. Thank God often for this.

Close in prayer, thanking God for sending His Son and for promising to send Jesus once again.

The Future and the King

The Rapture: believers meeting Jesus in the air

Jesus' Second Coming

Ready and Waiting

Jesus wants us to be ready and waiting for His return. While we wait, He wants us to be doing His work. He gave commands to seven churches that were serving God when John wrote the Book of Revelation. They are found in Revelation chapters 2 and 3. The commands to these churches are for us today, too. After each command, write one way you can obey the command in your life.

Command to the Church	How I Will Obey the Command
The church in Ephesus: Keep your love for God fresh.	
The church in Smyrna: Be faithful during trials.	
The church in Pergamum: Repent of your sins.	
The church in Thyatira: Keep My commandments.	
The church in Sardis: Keep yourself pure from wrongdoing.	
The church in Laodicea: Be zealous for God, not lukewarm.	
The church in Philadelphia: Keep God's Word.	

Are you waiting for Jesus to come back?

Is His return exciting to you?

How are you showing God that you're waiting and ready for the return of the King?

Jesus and the Tabernacle

LESSON PLAN

OBJECTIVE: Students will reaffirm how God's plan, as revealed throughout the Bible, has always been to send His Son to die for our sins.

APPLICATION: Students will praise God for His Word and how it shows us His Son and brings us closer to Him.

LESSON PLAN ELEMENT	ACTIVITY	TIME	SUPPLIES
Opening Activity	*Taking a Tour*	10–15	Paper and pencils
Bible Story—Exodus 35—38, building the Tabernacle walls	*The Tabernacle, a Picture of Christ*	7–10	Bible; piece of white linen cloth; piece of brown fur; piece of lamb's wool dyed red; piece of gray fur; "The Tabernacle" handouts
Lesson Activity	*The Furniture, a Picture of Christ*	3–5	Bibles; "The Tabernacle" handouts; glue; scissors; two colors of yarn (red, blue, or purple); paper; markers
Memory Verse Activity	*Worship Recitation*	7–10	Dry-ease marker or chalk; "The Tabernacle" handouts; pencils
Application	*The Tabernacle, the Picture of Our Lives*	7–10	"The Tabernacle" handouts; pencils; student drawings from the Opening Activity (optional)
Check for Understanding	*Time Line Review*	3–5	Complete time line and all the pictures from previous lessons; 1 copy of "The Tabernacle" master; tape
Weekly Assignment	*God Dwells With Us Today*	3–5	Bible; "The Tabernacle" handouts

Why is a lesson on the Tabernacle the review lesson in this book? Because the Tabernacle reminds us about the most important parts of the Christian life. And the Tabernacle represents the Lord Jesus Christ, who is the central Person of the Bible. In studying the Tabernacle, your students will hear a summary of the main themes of the Bible.

The Tabernacle and its furnishings have many lessons for us. Examine the following diagram. Notice the three sections in the Tabernacle: the large area of service, the Holy Place, and the Holy of Holies. Each area was hidden from the others by curtains. When Solomon built his temple after the Israelites had settled in the Promised Land, he followed the same pattern for the inner parts, carefully following God's instructions.

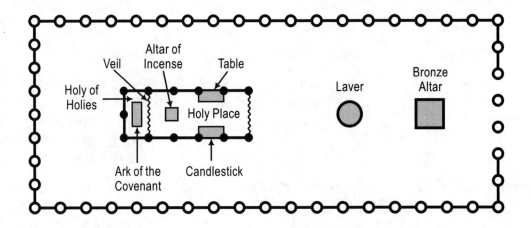

Note the pieces of furniture. The first is the Brazen Altar, which was used for sacrifice and atonement. Then came the Laver. It was used for cleansing.

As you proceed into the Holy Place, you will see the Table of Shewbread on the right; on the left is the Candlestick. Straight ahead is the Altar of Incense.

Beyond this Altar is the Veil of the Tabernacle that hid the Holy of Holies from the eyes of everyone except the High Priest. In the Holy of Holies we find the Ark, which was where God met with the people through the High Priest.

As you study this lesson, you will see how God prepared this Tabernacle, not just for worship and sacrifice, but also as an illustration of the Son He would send to earth. The Tabernacle had one door—just as Jesus is the only Way to the Father. The first act that a worshiper did when he entered the courtyard was to offer a sacrifice for his sins. That is also our first act as a believer: we ask Jesus to be the sacrifice for our sins. He paid the price so we can go in. The Laver represents the cleansing from sin that we need as we sin in our daily life. As we confess our sin, God cleanses us.

The Table of Shewbread points to Jesus as the Bread of Life. The Candlestick points to Jesus as the Light of the World. The Altar of Incense represents our prayers to God, which are our sweet-smelling offering to Him.

The Veil represents the fact that we cannot go into the holy presence of God because we are sinners. Only through the blood of Christ, which cleanses us from our sin, can we enter into God's presence. That's why at the crucifixion of Jesus Christ, the Veil in the temple was ripped in two by unseen hands. God was showing us that Jesus Christ's death provided the way for us to have access to God.

Inside the Holy of Holies was the Ark of the Covenant on which was the Mercy Seat. That is what God gives us, mercy. What a perfect picture of God's relationship with His people. We can be encouraged that God prepared the way for us to come into His presence long before we were even born.

As you teach this lesson, emphasize the continuity of the Scripture. Through explaining what the pieces of furniture represent, show how God was telling the story of His Son and how His people must come before Him in His Son's name.

LESSON PLAN

OPENING ACTIVITY: Taking a Tour

Before Class: Plan to take your students on a trip to your church's sanctuary or worship center. If this is not possible, take pictures of the pieces of furniture and places where activities occur within the service. Or bring pictures of other churches' sanctuaries.

Ask your students to explain how they feel about the return of Jesus when He comes to take believers to heaven. Discuss how their excitement about this future event has changed the way they look at their world and their desire to obey God.

Have your students form a line to walk to your church's sanctuary or worship center to look at how it is set up. Give your students pencil and paper to take with them to write down what they see. Point out things such as communion table, raised platform, cross, and pulpit. As you point out each item, discuss how it is used. Encourage students to draw sketches of what they see.

When you return to your classroom, allow students to show their drawings and describe what they are.

BIBLE STORY: The Tabernacle, a Picture of Christ

So far in our study about God's Word, we have learned that Jesus is the central Person of the Bible. The Bible is God's message to us, telling us what we should do, how we should relate to God, and what we should avoid doing. The Bible also gives us a picture of who God is and how much He loves us. He proved His love by sending His Son, Jesus, to die for our sins.

The New Testament tells the story of Jesus and how He arose from the dead. It also tells us about the new church that Jesus entrusted to the apostles that eventually reached around the world.

The Old Testament also tells us about Jesus, but there He is called the Messiah, the Sent One. The prophets foretold of His coming. Many of the stories in the Old Testament point to what Jesus would do for His people in the future.

Just imagine that you were with the Israelites as they left Egypt, crossed the Red Sea, and headed into the desert. This was a difficult change for them. They were used to living in homes in Egypt, eating Egyptian food. Now all they could see was the desert.

But God was with them. He was taking care of them and protecting them. He told Moses to build a Tabernacle so that the people would always know that He was with them.

The Tabernacle is a picture of Jesus Christ. As we study what the Tabernacle looked like and what was in it, we will see that it teaches us lessons about God's Son.

When Moses came to Mount Sinai in the desert, he went to the mountaintop to get the Ten Commandments from God. But something else happened. Moses was also given the instructions on how to build the Tabernacle.

But how would the people find the items necessary to build the Tabernacle? After all, they were out in a desert where they didn't have anything to gather.

Moses commanded the people to bring what they had in their possession. And they did! **Read Exodus 35:4–9,20–29; 36:1–7.**

The people were so excited about the Tabernacle that they brought more than enough to do the work. Moses had to tell them to quit bringing their gold and silver because the workers had more than they needed!

God told Moses exactly how to build the Tabernacle. **Distribute the "Tabernacle" handouts.** On the outside was a fence made of pure white linen. **Point out the outside perimeter (fence) on the handout. Pass around the white cloth for your students to touch.** This fence reminded the people of the purity and righteousness of God.

Inside the fence was the Tabernacle covering. The covering was taller than the fence so everyone standing outside could see the covering over the fence.

You would think that God would have made this covering very beautiful. But He didn't. The outside that everyone could see was made of brown badger skin. **Point out the Tabernacle perimeter on the handout. Pass around the brown piece of fur.**

- Why do you think this covering was so ordinary looking? *(Because God wanted to save the beautiful stuff for the inside. It was stronger.)*

The badger skin protected the Tabernacle from rain, wind, and sandstorms. But it also was a picture of what Jesus would look like when He came to earth. **Have a volunteer read Isaiah 53:2.** When Jesus came, many of the Jewish people did not recognize Him. He was not the glorious King they expected, but just a common Man. Like the plain brown badger skin, Jesus was not beautiful.

Underneath the badger's skin was a covering of red ram's skin. **Pass around the red wool.**

- What do you think this red ram's skin represented? *(The blood of the Lamb, Jesus Christ.)*

Under that was a third covering made of goat's hair. **Pass around the piece of gray fur.** Goats were sacrificed once a year to pay for the people's sin. Once again, this covering pictured what Jesus would do for His people.

Then there was a fourth covering underneath that. It was made of linen cloth, which was colored red, purple, and blue. It had cherubim (a type of angel) embroidered on it. Since it was the covering inside the Tabernacle, the priests could look up and see the cherubim. The cherubim reminded them of God's holiness.

The red color reminded them of blood. The purple is the color of royalty, in this case the King of kings. And the blue reminded them of heaven. All these colors pointed to Jesus.

- How does the red remind us of Jesus? *(He shed His blood for us.)*

- How does the purple remind us of Jesus? *(He is the King of kings.)*

- How does the blue remind us of Jesus? *(He came from heaven and He went back to heaven.)*

- If you had been one of the Israelites, what would you have liked to have done to help make the Tabernacle? *(I'd bring gold and silver and anything else I had. I'd like to help make the cloth for the fence and the coverings. I'd like to work with wood and gold and silver to make things for inside the Tabernacle.)*

- How is this like what God asks us to do today? *(He wants us to give Him part of what we own to do His work. He wants us to help build up His church.)*

Isn't it amazing that God instructed Moses to build a worship center that pointed the way to Jesus? But the outside of the Tabernacle was not the most interesting part. Inside were pieces of furniture that helped people understand God's plan, too. In our Lesson Activity, we'll look at them.

LESSON ACTIVITY: The Furniture, a Picture of Christ

Have students sit at a table so they can work on their handouts while you teach. Set out scissors, glue, markers, yarn, and paper. As you discuss each piece of furniture, have students cut it out of the handout and glue it to their "Tabernacles." You could also have students color or draw on each piece to make it more realistic. Use the string to represent the curtain or veil inside the tabernacle. Instruct students to work while you explain each piece. See the following drawing for the placement of all parts.

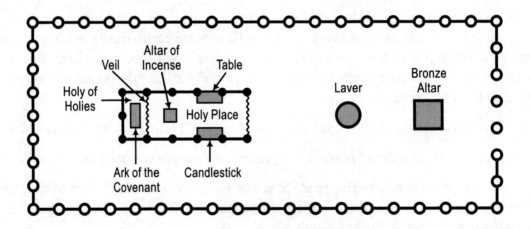

Inside the Tabernacle were three areas. We'll start with the area closest to the door and work our way inside.

The Tabernacle had only one door. **Point out the door on the handout.** This reminds us that Jesus is the Door, the only way to God. In John 10:9 Jesus said, "I am the door. If anyone enters by Me, he will be saved" (NKJ).

Right inside the door was the Bronze Altar. It was made of wood and covered with bronze, a brownish-colored metal. It was not very tall so that anyone could see over it. A fire was always kept burning in the altar.

Altar means "killing place." An Israelite had to bring a perfect live animal such as a lamb or bull to be sacrificed on the altar. The person would put his hands on the head of the animal to show that the animal was being sacrificed for his sins. The animal was to die in the place of its owner. Then the person would confess his sins.

Have a volunteer read Hebrews 10:4. Animal sacrifices had to be made over and over. But Jesus, the Lamb of God, made one sacrifice to pay for all sins.

No one could come into the Tabernacle without first confessing his sins.

- What does this show us about God's holiness? *(We cannot come to God without a sacrifice for our sins and confessing our sins.)*

Next was the Laver. **Point out the Laver.** It was made of bronze and you could see yourself in its reflection. In fact, it was made from the bronze mirrors that the women brought to Moses. (There were no glass mirrors back then; they were made of bronze.) The Laver was filled with water. After performing the sacrifice, the priest came to the Laver and washed his hands and his dusty feet. God said that if the priest came inside the Tabernacle without washing himself clean, he would die.

Now we come to the Holy Place. **Have your students cut a piece of one color of string and glue it on the "curtain" or box around the Candlestick and Table.** The curtain around the Holy Place kept everyone but the priests from looking in. The exciting part of this is that God calls us His priests. As Christians, we are cleansed from our sin so we are allowed to come into God's Holy Place.

Inside the Holy Place were three furnishings. On the left side was the Candlestick. **Point out the Candlestick.** It was beaten out of one piece of gold. It had three branches on each side and one in the middle for a total of seven. The cups on the branches held olive oil and burned all the time.

The Candlestick reminds us that Jesus is the Light of the world. **Have a volunteer read John 8:12.**

On the right was the Table. The priest placed twelve loaves of bread on it, one for each of the twelve tribes of Israel. The Table reminds us that Jesus is the Bread of Life. **Have a volunteer read John 6:35.**

Behind these two pieces was the Altar of Incense. **Point out this piece.** The Altar is the reminder of our prayers, which are like sweet-smelling smoke rising up to God.

Only the priests could trim the wicks on the Candlestick, put new loaves of bread on the Table, and offer incense on the Altar of Incense. They could only do this after they had been cleansed of their sins.

Then the priest came to a Veil. It divided the Holy Place from the Holy of Holies. **Have students glue the second color of string over the line dividing these two areas in the**

Tabernacle. The Veil was blue, purple, and red and had cherubim embroidered on it. It kept everyone out of the Holy of Holies except the High Priest. He was the only person allowed to go into the Holy of Holies, and he could go in only once a year. To go in, he had to bring a blood sacrifice.

Inside was only one piece of furniture, the Ark of the Covenant. It was a wooden box covered with gold inside and out. Inside the box were three items: Aaron's staff that had budded, a pot of manna that the people ate as they went through the wilderness, and the tablets with the Ten Commandments written on them. These articles reminded the High Priest that God takes care of His people.

On top of the Ark was the Mercy Seat. It was a slab of gold with two cherubim on each side looking down at it. They had their wings outspread. The Mercy Seat reminded the High Priest that God gives mercy to His people. On this seat, the High Priest put the offering of blood. That showed that God's mercy was given because of the blood of the sacrifice. Jesus was that sacrifice. He gave His blood so that we could have God's mercy.

Let's learn a memory verse to help us remember God's plan for saving us from our sin through Jesus Christ.

MEMORY VERSE ACTIVITY: Worship Recitation

Hebrews 10:10—"By that will, / we have been made holy / through the sacrifice / of the body of Jesus Christ / once for all."

Write the memory verse on the board as shown. Make sure students have their "The Tabernacle" handouts and pencils.

Read Hebrews 10:5–10. Our memory verse is Hebrews 10:10. **Reread that verse.** In this verse, "by that will" means by the will of God. In other words, God planned and determined to send His Son, Jesus, to become a sacrifice for us. Jesus came to earth in a body that God prepared for Him, and Jesus agreed to suffer and die in our place. So the sacrifices that the people did in the Tabernacle were not what pleased God. They really couldn't save anyone from sin. Instead, the sacrifices were only a picture of what would happen later on the cross. God was totally pleased with the sacrifice of Jesus.

Write the memory verse on the back of your "Tabernacle" handout. **Give students time to write.**

In some worship services, the pastor will recite parts of a verse while the congregation recites the other parts. Let's memorize our verse using this method. Let's do it in a worshipful way as we think about what God did for us on the cross.

Have students move their chairs so they are in rows like a worship service. Stand in front of the rows to lead this activity. Alternate reading the lines of the verses: you read the first line, the students read the second line, and so forth. Have students stand to recite their line, then sit again when their part is finished. If the standing tempts them to laugh or jump up and down, remind them to be worshipful. (You might want to use a chair yourself to help set the proper mood as you stand and sit.)

Recite the lines a few times. Then reverse the order so the students recite the first line and so forth. Then erase the verse and repeat the process until your students know the verse.

APPLICATION: The Tabernacle, the Picture of Our Lives

By using our Tabernacle, we can remember what God wants us to do in our Christian life. Let's write on our Tabernacles some ways we can worship God and obey Him.

Put a number 1 beside your Bronze Altar. Write down when you received Jesus as your Savior. It could be a date or a time such as "after church one day when I was nine years old." **Give students time to write.**

Now move to the Laver. When we sin as Christians, we must "wash" ourselves by confessing our sins to God. We do this through prayer. Put a number 2 beside the Laver. Write "I will be sure to confess my sin" beside the number. This is to remind you that you need to confess your sin as soon as the Holy Spirit brings it to your mind. **Give students a moment to write.**

Go to the Holy Place. As a believer in Jesus, you can enter into the Holy Place because Jesus has taken away all your sin with His blood. Write a 3 beside the Table. Jesus is the Bread of Life. In the Bible, bread also represents the Word of God. Write "I will read my Bible every day" beside the number 3. **Give students time to write.**

Now go to the Candlestick. Jesus is the Light of the World. We are also supposed to be lights for Jesus by telling others about how He died to save them from their sins. Write a number 4 next to the Candlestick. Beside the 4, write "I will tell others about Jesus." **Give students time to write.**

Now go to the Altar of Incense. That reminds us that we need to pray many times a day. Write the number 5 by the Altar of Incense, and beside it write "I will talk to God." **Give students time to write.**

As a child of God, you can also go into the Holy of Holies. This is an awesome place. This is where we remember what Jesus did for us. It also reminds us that God takes care of us. (Remember that the Ark held Aaron's staff, a pot of manna, and the Ten Commandments tablets.) Put a number 5 next to the Ark. Beside it, write "I will thank God for what He has done for me." **Give students time to write.**

> *Optional Activity:* Have students take out their drawings from the Opening Activity and discuss how the items in your worship center point us to Jesus Christ. (For example, the communion table reminds us of the body and blood of Jesus; the pulpit is where Christ's message is preached; the cross represents Jesus' death and resurrection.)

CHECK FOR UNDERSTANDING: Time Line Review

 Before Class: Make another copy of "The Tabernacle" handout. Cut out the pieces of furniture and the Tabernacle outline.

Tape the Tabernacle shape on the time line, above the "Moses Receiving the Ten Commandments" picture, to give students an idea of when the Tabernacle was built. Review the history of man from the beginning to the end, bringing out the different eras: creation, the Patriarchs, the nation of Israel, the coming of Jesus, the beginning of the church, and the future coming of Jesus.

Hold up each piece of furniture, and have a student tell what it is and tape it where it goes within the Tabernacle walls.

WEEKLY ASSIGNMENT: God Dwells With Us Today

Review the names of the Old and New Testament books.

Have students record their daily reading assignments in their Bible Reading Journals:

Day 1—Exodus 35
Day 2—Exodus 36
Day 3—Exodus 37
Day 4—Exodus 38
Day 5—Hebrews 10
Day 6—Psalm 91
Day 7—Psalm 139

Have students sit in a circle. Spend a few moments praising God for making His home in our hearts. Explain that we are His Tabernacle today and what an awesome privilege and responsibility this is. Read Psalm 93 and use it to praise God.

Before your students leave, make sure they have their "Tabernacle" handouts. Suggest that they display their work in their bedrooms and use it to help them walk with God each day. Encourage your students to keep growing in Christ.

If you are going to continue to Book 4 of the Children's Disciples Series (*Building an Active Faith*), show them your teacher's book cover and mention some of the exciting things they will be learning.

The Tabernacle

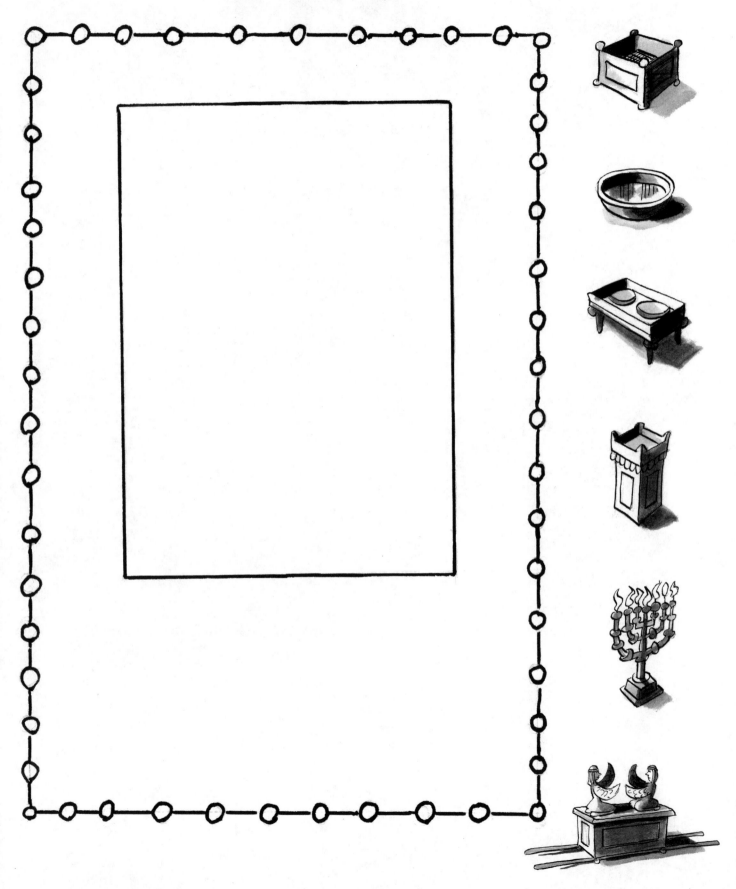

Resources

"THE STORY OF JESUS FOR CHILDREN" VIDEO

This 62-minute video entertains, educates, and introduces children to the life of Jesus of Nazareth, giving them a chance to see and hear the whole story of Jesus at once! The video answers questions in clear and concrete terms, provides fast action, and ends with an invitation, by a child to children, to choose to invite Jesus into their lives. Children of all ages will enjoy this captivating retelling of the true story of Jesus from a child's perspective.

THE GREATEST PROMISE

The Greatest Promise booklet is developed especially for children. Complete with Scripture references, illustrations from the *JESUS* film, and more. This is a great follow-up tool for use after the video. One copy of *The Greatest Promise* booklet comes free with every *The Story of Jesus for Children* video.

To order additional copies, contact The JESUS Film Project at 800-432-1997.

RESURRECTION EGGS: THE EASTER STORY FOR CHILDREN
Randall Lee Walti

Twelve colorful eggs contain symbols that illustrate events in the death, burial, and resurrection of Jesus. An easy-to-understand booklet explains how to use these Resurrection Eggs®, and Bible stories reveal the significance of each object.

To order, contact FamilyLife at 800-FL-TODAY or visit www.familylife.com.

WOULD YOU LIKE TO BELONG TO GOD'S FAMILY?
Bill Bright
(ISBN 1-56399-081-4)

The popular and practical *Four Spiritual Laws* is now available in a fun, illustrated format kids can read and understand. Designed for elementary-aged children, *Would You Like to Belong to God's Family?* presents the gospel as four facts (rather than four laws) to help them learn how to become members of God's family through faith in Jesus Christ.

THE GOOD NEWS COMIC
Bill Bright
(ISBN 1-56399-094-6)

Help children understand who God is in a simple and relevant way with this fun, colorful gospel story in comic book form—a favorite children's ministry tool for decades! Ideal for Sunday school and vacation Bible school, or as bag stuffers for Halloween or birthday parties.

THE GOOD NEWS GLOVE
Bill Bright
(ISBN 1-56399-074-1)

A classic and fun witnessing tool, this colorful glove helps children understand and remember the gospel. Each finger communicates a basic spiritual truth in an exciting, game-like fashion that captures kids' attention and hearts. Use it alone or with *The Good News Comic*.

IN SEARCH OF THE GREATEST TREASURE
Bill Bright
(ISBN 1-56399-120-9)

Join a delightful band of children as they embark on a treasure hunt…not for buried treasure, but for the greatest person who ever lived. Written in comic-book fashion, this brightly-colored, easy-to-use booklet helps children understand who Jesus is and why He is the Greatest Treasure.

A CHILD OF THE KING
Bill Bright and Marion R. Wells
(ISBN 1-56399-150-0)

A Child of the King is a timeless tale of a kingdom turned away from the sun, a brave but vulnerable orphan, a diabolical foe and a king whose love never ends. The story could be your own. Perhaps it is.

Written in the beloved, allegorical tradition of C. S. Lewis' *Chronicles of Narnia* and J. R. R. Tolkien's *The Lord of the Rings*, *A Child of the King* takes you on a quest for truth, virtue, and self-worth in a dark and hostile world. Share the adventures of Jotham, the People of the Book, and others in the Kingdom of Withershins…and realize your own high calling as a child of the King.

HAVE YOU MADE THE WONDERFUL DISCOVERY OF THE SPIRIT-FILLED LIFE?
Bill Bright
(ISBN 1-56399-020-2)

Discover the reality of the Spirit-filled life and how to live in moment-by-moment dependence on Him. Millions have learned to live the abundant life that Christ promises by following the simple, biblical truths found in this booklet. Use the booklet to refresh your own walk with Christ or to share with others.

These and other fine products from *NewLife* Publications are available from your favorite bookseller or by calling (800) 235-7255 (within U.S.) or (407) 826-2145, or by visiting www.newlifepubs.com.

Certificate

This certificate is awarded to:

for successfully completing "Growing in God's Word,"
Book 3 of the Children's Discipleship Series

CHURCH AND CITY

DATE

NAME, POSITION

NAME, POSITION